THE 40 DAY PRAYER CHALLENGE™

*Unlocking the Power
of Partnered Prayer*

SQUIRE RUSHNELL
& LOUISE DUART

Official Guide to
The 40 Day Prayer Challenge™

 HOWARD BOOKS
An Imprint of Simon & Schuster, Inc.

NEW YORK   NASHVILLE   LONDON   TORONTO   SYDNEY   NEW DELHI

Howard Books
An Imprint of Simon & Schuster, Inc.
1230 Avenue of the Americas
New York, NY 10020

First Howard Books trade paperback edition January 2017

HOWARD and colophon are trademarks of Simon & Schuster, Inc.

For information about special discounts for bulk purchases, please contact Simon & Schuster Special Sales at 1-866-506-1949 or business@simonandschuster.com.

The Simon & Schuster Speakers Bureau can bring authors to your live event. For more information or to book an event, contact the Simon & Schuster Speakers Bureau at 1-866-248-3049 or visit our website at www.simonspeakers.com.

Manufactured in the United States of America

10 9 8 7 6 5 4 3 2 1

The Library of Congress has cataloged the hardcover edition as follows:

Rushnell, Squire D., 1938–
    The 40 day prayer challenge: unlocking the power of partnered prayer / SQuire Rushnell, Louise DuArt.
        pages   cm
    Includes bibliographical references and index.
    1. Married people—Religious life.   2. Prayer—Christianity.   I. Title.
        BV4596.M3R875   2016
        248.3'p208655—dc23   2015026510

ISBN 978-1-5011-1967-5
ISBN 978-1-5011-2707-6 (pbk)
ISBN 978-1-5011-1968-2 (ebook)

This book supports a national movement led by Pray Together, Stay Together, Inc., a 501(c)(3) nonprofit that is working in association with American churches to restore relationships and revitalize families through the supernatural power of Partnered Prayer.

The 40 Day Prayer Challenge also parallels the first-ever empirical study, conducted by Baylor University's Institute for Studies of Religion, measuring the phenomenal outcomes when two people pray together five minutes a day, for forty days.

AUTHORS' NOTE

THE 40 DAY PRAYER CHALLENGE . . .

is formed on the foundation of this challenge
from the ancient Scriptures:

When my people humble themselves **[That's YOU]**—
the ones who are called by my name—
and PRAY and SEEK me **[That's YOUR challenge]**,
and turn away from their evil practices **[You can do that]**,
I MYSELF WILL LISTEN from heaven
[He's listening to YOUR PRAYERS],
I will PARDON their sins, and I will RESTORE their land
[That is YOUR PROMISE].
—2 Chronicles 7:14, ISV

Right now you are standing at the tipping point to the rest of
your life! Join the movement of hundreds of thousands who are
discovering that Partnered Prayer increases the power of prayer
by many multiples—a supernatural phenomenon!

—SQuire & Louise

CONTENTS

CHAPTER 3: PARTNERED PRAYER

A. COUPLES

B. FAMILIES

INTRODUCTION

DEFINITION

Partnered Prayer [pärt'nər'd•prer] noun
1. The actions of two people—married or non-married couples; two family members; or two friends—who have agreed to pray together in partnership.

THE 40 DAY PRAYER CHALLENGE

This book is designed to guide you and a partner through The 40 Day Prayer Challenge to develop your daily habit of *speaking together* with God. In so doing, you are unwrapping a special gift that has been awaiting you in these ancient words: "Whatever you ask for in prayer, *believe* that you have received it, and it will be yours."[1]

The premise is this: if you and your spouse, family member, or friend are willing to commit to as little as five minutes a day, speaking with God about issues of concern to you, and praising Him for blessings you've experienced since yesterday—much the same as two people would gather with a granddad over a cup of tea and a biscuit for a daily chat—the joy in your life will expand immeasurably.

Our beta-study evidence impressively demonstrates that when two people are willing to spend five minutes a day—as much time as you spend combing your hair and brushing your teeth— coming before the very Creator who has given you life on earth, *speaking* of concerns and matters from the heart, *believing* God will not let you down, and *expecting* the outcome you have asked for, your lives will change for the better forever.

"Change for the better forever."

Your prayer, particularly when you *speak it together* with a partner, will lift the veil between here and Heaven, and draw not only God's attention, but His delight.

In my distress . . . I prayed to my God for help.
He heard me from his sanctuary;
my cry . . . reached his ears.
—PSALMS 18:6, NLT

RARE RESEARCH ON PRAYER

In our earlier book, *Couples Who Pray*, we introduced Gallup data that was evaluated by Baylor University's prestigious Institute for Studies of Religion. The rudimentary research provided evidence of surprising levels of improvement when two people went from "praying sometimes" to "praying a lot."

Keeping in mind that most mates *never* pray together, you will see why George Gallup considered this cursory data astonishing:

- Happiness elevated by 18 percent
- Agreement on raising children up by 11 percent
- Agreement on financial matters increased by 11 percent
- Compromise rose 22 percent
- Communication went up by 11 percent
- Respect was higher by 19 percent
- Feelings of delight rocketed to 30 percent
- Lovemaking soared by 20 percent
- Marital stability became 16 percent greater
- The fear of divorce plummeted to zero

In concert with this book—and hopefully with you and your prayer partner—Baylor University's Institute for Studies of Religion will evaluate the data from a new study—the first empirical study of its kind—which measures the outcome of two people praying together, for at least five minutes a day, for forty days. More information is available at PrayStay.org.

The data will be gathered digitally on smartphones, tablets, and computers in a ten-minute survey that you and your partner will take on your first and fortieth days of praying together. Your private information will be unseen by anyone except social scientists at Baylor.

At the end of your forty days you'll have a report card in the form of bar graphs on how well you have done in many of the same measurements that were indicated in the Gallup study above.

Are you willing to open your gift and take this wondrous journey with us? Are you prepared to wake up every day excited and energized to see what the God of heaven and earth has in store for you?

Get ready. It's more than you could imagine.

CHAPTER 1

HOW PARTNERED PRAYER WORKS

SPEAK IT! BELIEVE IT! EXPECT IT!

Everything that exists comes from God *speaking it* into existence.

He spoke, "Let there be light" . . . and there was.

He spoke, "Let us make mankind" . . . and He did.[1]

God began everything with the awesome power of the *spoken* word, and He beckons you to emulate Him through a magnificent gift that is delivered through your lips and the passion in your heart. His promise is in the Bible: "Whatever you *ask* in prayer, *believing*, you shall *receive*."[2]

Let's look at the key words to opening your gift: first, to *ask in prayer*—through the power of the *spoken* word; second, to *believe* that God is who He says He is and can do what He says He can do; and third, to *expect* to *receive* "whatsoever ye shall ask in prayer."

How do you assure that your prayer reaches God's attention? You *speak* it!

When you learn to *speak* it, you hurtle every prayer through time and space directly to the ears of God. Like an arrow placed in the archer's bow, when you *speak* it, your prayer gains trajectory and velocity to the Almighty. And when you engage with a partner to pull back on the bowstring—to *speak it together*—the words of your prayer can move heaven and earth!

> *The tongue has the power of life and death.*
> —PROVERBS 18:21

THE MIRACLES OF CHRIST WERE SPOKEN INTO BEING

When Jesus looked at the two blind men and said, "Do you believe I can do this?" they replied, "Yes, Lord."

Jesus then *spoke* these words: "According to your faith, let it be done." And the blind men were healed.[3]

When a great storm alarmed the disciples in the boat, Jesus said, "Why are you afraid, you men of little faith?"[4] Then He rebuked the winds and the sea . . . He *spoke* to them . . . and they became perfectly calm.

When Jesus came upon two violent, demon-possessed men, He *spoke* to them, saying, "Go!"[5] The demons came out, went into the swine, and perished in the sea.

Christ *spoke* miracles into being.

THE THREE KEYS TO YOUR PRAYERS BEING ANSWERED

The first two keys to unlocking God's promise to you are: *speaking* prayer fervently and *believing* that God hears your every request. But the third key is equally essential: *expecting* your prayer will be answered, sometimes before you have even finished speaking or before your request has come into existence.

The Ancient Scriptures of Isaiah affirm "Before they call, I will answer; and while they are yet *speaking*, I will hear."[6]

In Romans we are assured that God "calls into existence things that don't yet exist."[7]

Christ confirmed those promises: "Whoever . . . does not doubt in his heart, but believes what God says is going to happen, it will be granted him."[8]

Therefore, how does effective prayer work? *Speak it. Believe it. Expect it!*

Jesus reiterates: "Therefore I tell you, whatever you ask for in prayer, believe that you have received it, and it will be yours."[9]

THE MIRACLES OF TODAY ARE SPOKEN INTO BEING

In this book you will see how *speaking* words of prayer, in faith, will plug you into the greatest power strip in the universe.

You will read how a mother *spoke* life over the body of her fourteen-year-old son, dead for nearly an hour, with the words, "Holy Spirit, give me back my son," and suddenly a doctor shouted, "We've got a pulse!"

How an unseen voice spoke to a mother in Vermont, commanding her to stand during her pastor's sermon and boldly *speak out* to ask for immediate prayer for her son, a soldier in Iraq, and for her to later learn that her son was supernaturally dodging a deadly bullet at that very moment.

How a woman forcefully *spoke* scripture to a man who was

holding her at gunpoint. He suddenly turned around, walked away, and subsequently said his getting caught was a "God thing."

How a child's daily prayers to have a pet bird, *spoken* in earnest, and with faith, were answered by a stranger, out of the blue.

How a dilapidated church of twenty people, about to close its doors, *spoke out together* in fervent prayer and, soon thereafter, crowds came through the doors, growing it into one of the largest, most prestigious churches in America.

Story after story will confirm that when you *speak* a prayer to God in faith—especially when you *speak it together* with a partner— you can tap into a limitless reservoir of spiritual promises.

You will be astonished by evidence of how the supernatural comes into the natural, overcoming your most insurmountable obstacles, as it did with a Florida cardiologist who, after pronouncing a man dead of a heart attack, heard a voice from God telling him to *speak* specific words of prayer over the man.

CHAUNCEY CRANDALL: A DOCTOR'S EVIDENCE THAT PRAYER WORKS

"I prayed for the dead man and today he's alive."

There was stunned silence throughout the medical conference as Dr. Chauncey Crandall, the noted cardiologist, unveiled compelling evidence that he had prayed for a patient who had just died and, as the man was being prepped for the morgue, came back to life.

The renowned Florida cardiologist was speaking to 120 physicians, representing fifty countries.

"The fifty-three-year-old man had had a massive heart attack. The medical team worked on him for over forty minutes . . . then declared him dead," said Dr. Crandall.[10] Having been called in to evaluate the patient toward the end, Dr. Crandall confirmed the man was dead. The doctor turned and started to leave.

Then, something odd happened.

"The Holy Spirit told me, 'Turn around and pray for that man.'"

Dr. Crandall walked back to the side of the bed, noting that the man's face, feet, and arms were completely black with death. Aloud, he prayed, "Lord Father, how am I going to pray for this man? He's dead. What can I do?"

Then, as if by supernatural means, words moved through the doctor's lips: "I cry out for the soul of this man if he does not know you as his Lord and Savior: raise him from the dead now, in Jesus' name."

> "The Holy Spirit told me . . . pray for that man."

Dr. Crandall told the spellbound audience at the conference that all of sudden a heartbeat showed up on the monitor. It was a perfect, normal beat, and then the man's fingers and toes started to move and he began mumbling words!

The nurse was startled. "Doctor Crandall, what have you done to this patient?"

The doctor calmed the nurse, then rushed the patient to intensive care, where, he says, "after a couple of days, he had an amazing story to tell."

The man told how he was in a dark place. There was no light. He felt as though he'd been thrown in the trash, worthless.

Dr. Crandall said he looked into the eyes of the man, explained the salvation message, and prayed with him. The man held out his hand and accepted Christ as his savior, as tears rolled from his eyes.

The doctor added tenderly, "You will never be thrown into the trash, into total darkness. . . . The light of the kingdom of Heaven is on you now."

Later, it was learned that the man had been estranged from his family for twenty years, yet they had never stopped praying for him. Even his ex-wife prayed for her ex-husband to come to know the Lord.

Everyone involved—the man, Dr. Crandall, the nurse, and most of the conference attendees—will all attest: prayer works!

The Spirit helps us in our weakness.
We do not know what we ought to pray for,
but the Spirit himself intercedes . . .
with the will of God.
—ROMANS 8:26

THE ROLE OF THE HOLY SPIRIT

Dr. Crandall said, "The Holy Spirit told me to 'turn around and to pray for that man.'" What did he mean by that?

He was literally receiving what Jesus described to his disciples. "The Holy Spirit, whom the Father will send in my name, will teach you all things and will remind you of everything." [11]

"Even when you don't know the right words to pray, the Holy Spirit prays with, and for you, and God answers," explains a concordance of the Bible.[12] When that happens, "He will guide you . . . empower you, protect you and reveal things to you." [13]

Evidence of that can be found in many of the stories in this book, stories about people who were guided, like Dr. Crandall, by the Holy Spirit.

It is comforting to know that the scriptures promise that the Holy Spirit is always with you to:

- warn you (Acts 20:23)
- assure you (Romans 8:16)
- convict you (John 16:8–11)
- direct you (Acts 20:22)
- guide you (Romans 8:14)
- strengthen you (Romans 8:26)
- empower you (John 16:12–15)

You can think of the Holy Spirit as your inner compass that keeps you from getting lost: your GPS—God's Positioning System. He adjusts your position and points you in the right direction.

If you are wondering if you should take that job, marry that person, or move to a different location, the Holy Spirit is the manifestation of God within you providing guidance, sometimes with a "nudge."

Some say that when they ask the Holy Spirit to speak to them, they will read the Bible and a particular passage will stand out as if the Bible had ears and was listening to them.

What no eye has seen, what no ear has heard,
and what no human mind has conceived . . .
these are the things God has revealed to us
by his Spirit.
—1 CORINTHIANS 2:9–10, NIV

WHY SHOULD I PRAY?

Consider these reasons:

- You have a deep-seated desire for something.
- You crave certainty and direction in your life.
- You secretly wish for a worry-free day.
- You've always wanted an incredible marriage.
- You yearn for a loving, trusting relationship with your children and family.
- Your quest to live longer and have financial security seems unattainable.
- You have a constant hurt—physical or emotional—that just won't go away.

If you identified even one of the above, you have just given yourself abundant grounds to *speak* to God in prayer.

IS THERE PROOF PRAYER WORKS?

There is massive evidence—biblical and scientific—that prayer not only works, but also elevates happiness and contentment in wondrous ways.

Prayer is so important that the Bible mentions it 512 times.

Prayer is so important that Jesus did nothing without it.

Prayer is so important that it's a command in the Ancient Scriptures.

Pray continually, give thanks in all circumstances;
for this is God's will for you in Christ Jesus.
—I THESSALONIANS 5:16, NIV

The Bible also promises that when you enter into Partnered Prayer, supernatural power expands.

> *Where two or three are gathered in my name*
> *I am there among them.*
> —MATTHEW 18, NIV

Words take flight when *spoken* sincerely, *believing* that they will "not come back void"[14] from God, and with the *expectation* that what you have just asked for is already done.

> *So shall my word be that goeth forth*
> *out of my mouth:*
> *it shall not return unto me void,*
> *but it shall accomplish that which I please,*
> *and it shall prosper in the thing whereto I sent it.*
> —ISAIAH 55:11, KJV

Jesus said that a speck of faith—the mere size of a mustard seed—is all you need to *speak out* at the mountains of worry and uncertainty that loom over you. And when you say, "Move from here to there,"[15] they will move!

When you *speak it* into existence, your prayer takes off with a supernatural lifting force, defying all reasoning of the human mind that might otherwise say that your prayers will fall to the ground. But when you *expect it* to be fulfilled, you can have Christ's promise: "Nothing will be impossible to you."[16]

Louise
THE WONDER-WORKING POWER OF FAITH

The Bible tells us that God *spoke* things into being. But we're told that *we* also have the power in us to *speak* things into being.

Really? We have that much power?

Yes. But our power isn't in ourselves, it's in God. Jesus tells us that there is wonder-working power when we have the faith to call upon God by *speaking* His words into a situation. He's always got you covered as long as you're resting not "on human wisdom, but on God's power." [17]

As mentioned above, Christ talked about having the faith to move mountains—meaning all the mountains in each of our lives—firmly *believing* that they will move when you *speak* to them. But this is an important distinction: so often we pray for *God* to move our mountains. However, the Bible tells us that God has given *us* the power to move mountains.

We are told, "It is with your heart that you *believe* . . . and it is with your mouth that you profess your faith" [18] and *speak* your prayer.

Jesus said, "You will receive whatever you ask for in prayer, if you believe." [19] But He's not going to do what He's already asked *you* to do. And if he's asked you to do it, He will give you His power to accomplish it.

Wow!

This sheds new revelation on *speaking* to our problems, doesn't it? It brings new meaning to that old hymn that says, "There is pow'r, pow'r, wonder-working pow'r . . ." [20]

It also confirms that we must study the Word to be enlightened about God's plan for our lives.

When you reach out to hold the hand of another—a spouse, a family member, or a friend—doubling the power of the prayers you *speak*, astonishing outcomes will flow down upon you. Following are two stories that help illustrate that.

Jeff Winter: A Pastor's Confession— We Didn't Pray Together

Several years ago I became the pastor of a small, nondenominational church on the island of Martha's Vineyard off the coast of Massachusetts. Within days, my wife, Judy, and I met SQuire and Louise. A friendship began.

As we got to know them, we learned of their passion to encourage married couples to pray with one another. They had been challenging couples all across the country to take The 40 Day Prayer Challenge. SQuire and Louise believe that if a married couple covenants to pray with each other for five minutes a day, for forty days, it will develop a habit that can last a lifetime.

Knowing the importance of prayer, I decided that the members of my church, FaithMV, ought to participate in The 40 Day Prayer Challenge. I felt in my heart that if the married couples of this tiny congregation were praying with each other, their lives would be enriched and so would the church.

But . . . as a pastor, I was facing a sizable issue. Leading The 40 Day Prayer Challenge would mean that I also needed to get off the fence in my prayer life with Judy. *Yikes*, I said to myself, *I'm a pastor and I rarely pray with my wife.*

For too many years, our prayer life had been hit-or-miss. We generally prayed together only when there was a crisis or a major decision to be made. Otherwise, we prayed individually.

Of course, Judy and I prayed with our flock. We prayed at meals. But praying together was a rare experience.

I felt guilty. Although Judy and I had become one in the eyes of God when we were married, we were not becoming one in our spiritual life together. So I asked God to help me lay aside any matters of personal pride, and we accepted The 40 Day Prayer Challenge.

Almost immediately I began to experience a positive change in our relationship as we entered into the presence of God on a daily basis. I also learned that just as physical intimacy reaffirms my oneness with Judy, so does praying together.

When we pray as a couple, we are stripped bare emotionally. There is little room for pretense; we are not only communicating with God, but also with each other. I have discovered so much more about Judy as we share our prayer requests, and as I listen to her pray out loud, I hear her heart.

Many years ago, I learned that I couldn't change Judy and she couldn't change me. But God can change each of us if we invite Him to do so through prayer. No matter what struggles we encounter, if we keep praying together, I am certain that we'll see circumstances turn around.

That was evident when our younger son was experiencing the consequences of a number of wrong choices. Our prayer time not only bonded Judy and me closer together, but we saw God move mightily in our son's life, helping him reclaim his relationship with Jesus Christ.

Praying with Judy has brought God into the center of our marriage. He is the glue that holds us together, in the good times and the bad. When we are fresh out of love and patience with each other, God has an inexhaustible supply of each, ready and waiting for us to ask.

God's grace, power, and forgiveness have helped us to make a good marriage great. Praying together has made the difference.

—JEFF WINTER

Judy Winter: The View from the Pastor's Wife

Through the ups and downs of forty years of marriage, Jeff and I have changed a lot for the better. We're far from perfect—but we are living proof that by praying together, a married relationship can change.

The most obvious outcome of daily devotions and praying with each other is how wonderful our relationship has grown; it's better than ever. We really miss it when something comes up and we can't meet for this time.

Prayer also encourages conversation. We are more up to date with each other, individually and spiritually. As we pray, it is like we are *speaking* to God as well as ourselves. It's definitely a three-way experience.

Then there is the effect we have on others because of our visible excitement and enthusiasm about prayer. We've started a prayer ministry in our church. A novel idea? An oxymoron? Well, even if we should have done it before, we recognize the need to get others involved and committed.

Finally, I would say that practice makes perfect. Prayer is

easier and more spontaneous because we find it to be second nature.

—JUDY WINTER

Since we know he hears us . . .
he will give us what we ask for.
—1 JOHN 5 : 15, NIV

Tim and Kathy Keller: The Day of Wide Awakening

The highly respected founder and pastor of the Redeemer Presbyterian Church in New York City, Tim Keller, was brought to a life-changing insight by a request spoken by his wife, Kathy.[21]

For weeks after two planes collided with the World Trade Center on 9/11 and lowered a surreal darkness over Manhattan, Tim and Kathy—like most of us—lived in a bubble of depression. But for New Yorkers, it was much too close to home. The twisted rubble, the loss of lives, and the endless search for the remains of loved ones was but a cab ride away. Kathy's struggle was intensified by her affliction with Crohn's disease.

Initially, Kathy's proposal didn't seem nearly as momentous as it turned out to be. With almost childlike sincerity, she spoke to Tim but with the wisdom of a wife.

"My wife asked me to do something we had never had the self-discipline to do regularly. She asked me to pray with her every night. *Every* night," he said.

A pastor's busy life—like yours—is filled with people to see, things to do, problems to solve.

As Tim looked into Kathy's eyes, unidentifiable feelings of guilt—or perhaps reluctance—streamed through his consciousness.

Kathy then supported her proposition with Godly insight. "Imagine you were diagnosed with a lethal condition and the doctor told you that you would die unless you took a particular pill every night."

Tim was beginning to see where she was going.

"Would you forget?" she continued. "Would you not get around to it some nights? No—it would be so crucial, you wouldn't forget, you would never miss a dose."

Kathy's reasoning and unpretentious logic were so clear, he was left to wonder, *How could this have escaped me, a professional man of the cloth?*

Kathy's voice grew with fervor: "If we don't pray together to God . . . we're not going to make it. I'm certainly not. We *have* to pray; we can't just let it slip our minds."

Perhaps that moment for Tim Keller was like this very moment is for you. "The penny dropped." He admitted anything that was "a nonnegotiable necessity" was something they could do.

That was more than thirteen years ago. Tim and Kathy now can't recall a single day when they have missed praying together—sometimes, if necessary, by telephone. Their relationship, daily lives, and very existence have benefited from a simple concept that is redundantly uttered in the Bible and *spoken* by a fervent wife: pray together.

WHAT IS THE SCIENTIFIC EVIDENCE FOR PRAYER?

Two British researchers, Alex Bunn and David Randall,[22] set out to evaluate the efficacy of prayer and faith. There had been many studies done on prayer, but it was nearly impossible to arrive at a collective conclusion. Thousands of research documents were scattered across the globe, among scholarly books, reports, and papers.

> *"The average person of faith had a life expectancy seven years longer than that of those who didn't have faith."*

Bunn and Randall rounded up every scientific study they could get their hands on, narrowed them down to those on faith and health, and cross-referenced the results. They analyzed sixteen hundred documents, including one American study that evaluated twenty-one thousand people over a nine-year period.

The outcome was definitive: the average person of faith had a life expectancy *seven years longer* than that of those who didn't have faith.

Bunn and Randall found that the majority of studies also linked faith to the following beneficial outcomes:

- well-being, happiness, and life satisfaction
- hope and optimism
- purpose and meaning in life
- higher self-esteem
- better adaptation to bereavement
- greater social support and less loneliness
- lower rates of depression
- lower rates of suicide

- less anxiety, less psychosis, and fewer psychotic tendencies
- lower rates of alcohol and drug abuse
- less delinquency and criminal activity
- greater marital stability and satisfaction

Even skeptics have to admit that sixteen hundred research documents—81 percent of which point to positive outcomes from the application of faith and prayer—are pretty compelling evidence.

SCIENTISTS WHO SURPRISE US WITH THEIR BELIEFS

Sir Isaac Newton, one of the world's most prominent scientists of the 1600s, was also one of the most distinguished students of the Bible.

Newton's Law of Gravity explained to the world the principle behind motion of the planets, but it was his faith that led him to conclude, "This most beautiful system of the sun, planets and comets, could only proceed from the counsel and dominion of an intelligent and powerful Being." [23]

Some said Newton actually spent more time studying theology than science. That was difficult to confirm until massive writings on his extensive study of the Bible were uncovered only seventy-five years ago.

While Newton would caution that books of science and theology must not be intermingled, he firmly believed both were "bound together," as did other scientists, such as Copernicus, Kepler, Galileo, and Pascal. [24]

In fact, it may be surprising to learn the number of highly

accredited scientists who concur with those legendary pioneers—science and faith go hand in hand.

Francis Collins, director of the National Institutes of Health, is best known as the leader of the team who mapped the entire DNA sequence of the human body, the Human Genome Project, about which he said, "It is humbling to me . . . to realize we have caught the first glimpse of our own instruction book, known previously only to God." [25]

"We have caught the first glimpse of our own instruction book, known previously only to God."

Once an atheist, like some of his peers in the scientific community, Collins was challenged by a grandmother who asked him, "What do you believe?" [26]

He admitted, "I found myself with a combination of willful blindness and . . . arrogance, having avoided any serious consideration that God might be a real possibility." After picking up the challenge—exhaustively researching theology versus science—he concluded, "Faith in God now seemed more rational than disbelief." [27]

Today Collins believes that if God has created all things, including science, one does not have to choose between the two of them—they are compatible.

"I found great joy in being both a scientist studying the genome and a follower of Christ," he says. [28]

Collins believes that perhaps 40 percent of the scientific community now travels a similar path of coexistence between science and theology.

Frank Tipler, professor of mathematical physics, says, "Twenty years ago I was a convinced atheist. I never in my wildest dreams imagined that one day I would be writing a book purporting to show that the central claims of Judeo-Christian theology are in fact true; that these claims are straightforward deductions of the laws of physics as we now understand them."[29]

NASA's space pioneer Wernher von Braun observes, "The knowledge that man can choose between good and evil should draw him closer to his creator."[30] Braun, a WWII German rocket scientist who surrendered to America after the war because its people were "guided by the Bible,"[31] believes that man's "survival here and hereafter depends on his adherence to the spiritual rather than the scientific."

In making a case for a designer of the universe, Braun posited the two most powerful forces shaping our culture are science and religion. "It is as difficult for me to understand a scientist who docs not acknowledge the presence of a superior rationality behind the existence of the universe as it is to comprehend a theologian who would deny the advances of science."[32]

Apollo 14 astronaut Edgar Mitchell looked back from the moon and said, "When I saw the planet Earth floating in the vastness of space, the presence of divinity became almost palpable, and I knew that life in the universe was not just an accident."[33]

> *"Life in the universe was not just an accident."*

Nobel Laureate Arno Penzias, codiscoverer of the radiation afterglow, remarks, "In the absence of an absurdly improbable accident, the observations of modern science seem to suggest an underlying, one might say, supernatural plan."[34]

Astronomer Allan Sandage comments, "God, to me, is a mystery, but is the explanation for the miracle of existence—why there is something instead of nothing."[35]

The Bible shows the way to go to heaven,
not the way the heavens go.[36]
—GALILEO

SQuire
HOW DOES PRAYER WORK?

I have a very simple acceptance of the merits of prayer: I've seen it work in the lives of my family, over and over again. I can recount many times when God answered my prayers affirmatively against the few times I perceived Him not answering.

I know He *does* answer prayers, I just don't know *how* He does it.

Put simply, prayer *works*.

Of course, when we stop to think of it, we are surrounded by countless conveniences that work for us, every day, yet we haven't a clue *how* they work.

For example, you put a cup of water in the microwave for tea, push the buttons 1-3-0, and one minute and thirty seconds later, the machine dings. It's ready.

Do you know *how* that contraption made your beverage the perfect temperature?

An engineer could explain it, but most of us don't know how. It just works.

I spent forty years making network television programs. Do I know *how* television sends images of people flying invisibly through the air, causing them to show up on my TV?

No. TV just works. That's all the evidence I need.

And while I know that God *causes* prayer to work, I remain clueless as to *how* He goes about doing it.

When my life hung in the balance, as I talk about in chapter 2, prayer worked. That's all that matters.

SQuire
WHEN YOU PRAY, GODWINKS HAPPEN

It had never occurred to me that there was no word in the English language for "answered prayer."

Yet in her letter, one of my readers was using the term "godwink"—a word coined in my first *When God Winks* book for those "little coincidences that aren't coincidence"—to describe her own experience of an answered prayer.

Instead of saying, "I had my prayer answered," she simply said, "I had a godwink."

How perfect, I thought; God was *speaking* to me again—this time, through my readers to help shape our understanding of the concept of godwinks.

A few days later, a confirmation—a divinely aligned godwink—entered into my awareness. I came across this quote from a famous seventeenth-century theologian and scholar:

> *When I pray, "coincidences" happen,*
> *and when I don't, they don't.*[37]
> —SIR WILLIAM TEMPLE (1628–1699)

Sir William Temple, a highly influential and respected theological leader in his day, was validating that there indeed is a clear connection between "so-called coincidences" and prayer.

So the new word was birthed into our language and is finding its way into everyday speech and soon into dictionaries. It has two meanings:

god•wink

1. An event or experience, often identified as a coincidence, so astonishing that it could only have come from God.
2. Another term for answered prayer.

MARTIN LUTHER KING JR.: WORDS ARE INVISIBLE YET INVINCIBLE

The Bible tells you, "Put on the full armor of God, so that you will be able to stand firm against the schemes of the devil." [38]

Your words, delivered with sincerity and faith, are the greatest weapons in your arsenal as you put on your armor. When *spoken* to the Almighty, they can heal a body and pull you from the depths of despair.

Words, when passionately *spoken*, can also lift hearts and alter the course of a nation.

Think about the extraordinary impact of words *spoken* by leaders that have resonated through the years. "Ask not what your country can do for you, but what you can do for your country," [39] in the inaugural address of President John F. Kennedy, ignited encouragement. A few years later his brother Robert Kennedy inspired us with, "There are those who look at things the way they are, and ask why . . . I dream of things that never were, and ask why not?" [40]

Then there were the first words *spoken* from the moon by Neil Armstrong, ushering in a new era of space exploration: "One small step for man, one giant leap for mankind." [41]

Yet no words more deeply pierced the hearts of millions and raised the hopes of everyone committed to freedom and equality than those that were improvised by Martin Luther King Jr. from the steps of the Lincoln Memorial in the summer of 1963.

The four words that provided a nation with a promissory note for healing were, "I have a dream." But those words were not written into Dr. King's prepared address handed out to the press.

That phrase had been uttered without prominence by MLK in two prior speeches, but on that day in DC, he had no plan to use it. How it got there, however, is quite a godwink.

As Martin Luther King Jr. looked out upon a sea of faces that were searching desperately for hope, he came to the end of a sentence that didn't quite feel right. At that very second, he heard the voice of Mahalia Jackson rise above the crowd.

"Tell them about the dream, Martin!" she shouted out to him.[42]

The words left her lips and, in a millisecond, triggered something in his mind. He said in a later interview that her comment instantly reminded him of that phrase, "I have a dream," and he said, "I just felt that I wanted to use it here."

Without missing a beat, his next line was: "I say to you today, my friends, so even though we face the difficulties of today and tomorrow, I still have a dream."

Then he began punctuating several sentences with those words, his voice rising in a slight tremor.

"I have a dream that my four little children will one day live in a nation where they will be judged not by the color of their skin, but by the content of their character."

He stirred emotions by concluding, "This will be the day when all God's children will be able to sing, 'From every mountainside, let freedom ring.'" And he closed with inspiring words from an old spiritual, "Free at last, free at last. Thank God Almighty, we are free at last."

That speech was judged to be the very top speech of the twentieth century by a poll of public speaking scholars in 1999.

Perhaps Mahalia Jackson is but a footnote in history, but her shouting out "Tell them about the dream, Martin!" at that divinely aligned moment caused her to be a "Godwink Link" for MLK, connecting him with the words God wanted him to *speak*. At the end of the day, we have to wonder, was that *her* motivation, or was that the voice of God speaking through her?

The God of glory thunders . . .
the voice of the Lord is powerful;
the voice of the Lord is majestic.
—PSALMS 29:3–4, NIV

CHAPTER 2

HOW TO PRAY

A MAN WITH A SIMPLE QUESTION

A large man in his fifties moved toward the platform. We had just wound up our presentation on what happens when two people pray together regularly.

As we have seen many times, couples, family members, and friends are fascinated with this concept that is so simple, yet so foreign to many. They always look astonished as they hear the stories of marriages revitalized by praying together.

They often wonder, *Why isn't this talked about more?*

The big man was now standing close by, waiting for someone to stop talking with us. Then he saw his opportunity.

Speaking tentatively, the man introduced himself as Ron, an Oklahoma City fireman who volunteered at the church.

"May I ask you a question?"

We nodded and leaned closer.

"How do you do it?"

Perhaps the blank looks on our faces were the clues he needed to tell us more.

"I pray alone . . . my wife prays alone . . . but how do you pray with somebody else? Are there special words you say? A place you should go?"

Those questions, almost childlike from a grown man—a churchgoer—led us to understand that we cannot take for granted that everyone knows *how* to pray *with another person* in Partnered Prayer.

But, before tackling that, there's a more basic question: Do you know how to pray by *yourself*?

That may seem like an elementary inquiry if you assume everyone knows how to pray, the way you know how to breathe or walk.

So, let's begin our discussion about Partnered Prayer by evaluating what we know about praying alone. You'll see that many of the same principles apply to both.

Do You Recall When Someone *Taught* You to Pray?

Was it a parent who tutored you?

A pastor? A teacher? A friend?

Like many of us, your answer might be, "No. I can't recall anyone *ever* teaching me *how* to pray."

That is a sad fact. We are often self-taught, emulating others who may speak out at group gatherings or someone we've seen on TV.

As result, like the man who approached us in Oklahoma City, there is an innocent uncertainty about Partnered Prayer and even praying alone. What words do I speak to the Almighty God? Do I have to use formal language? And isn't He much too busy dealing with all the other matters in the universe to have time for me?

When I pray with someone else, do I need to talk out loud or can I pray silently? What are the guidelines?

Suddenly all these questions make you feel inhibited.

The aim of this chapter is to deal with the basics: how to pray with a *partner*. But in most cases, these principles apply to praying *alone*, too.

DO YOU FEEL EMBARRASSED FOR EVEN ASKING HOW TO PRAY?

Don't beat yourself up. Even the disciples didn't know how to pray. One of them said, "Lord, teach us to pray." [1]

Subsequently, Jesus demonstrated what we now know as The Lord's Prayer.[2] He replied, "When you pray, say this . . ."

> *Our Father who art in heaven,*
> *hallowed be thy name.*
> *Thy kingdom come.*
> *Thy will be done,*
> *on earth as it is in heaven.*
> *Give us this day our daily bread.*
> *And forgive us our trespasses,*
> *as we forgive those who trespass against us.*
> *Lead us not into temptation,*
> *but deliver us from evil.*
> *For thine is the kingdom and the power and the glory forever.*
> *Amen.*

ACTS IS HELPFUL IN LEARNING TO PRAY

Our friends Dean and Kim Farmer remind us that the ACTS model is a helpful guide to prayer. ACTS stands for Adoration, Confession, Thanksgiving, and Supplication.

Adoration: This is focusing on who God is. Examples of adoration include statements like "God, You are the creator of the universe" or "Great and awesome God . . ."

Confession: This is when you tell God about the sins you have committed and ask for forgiveness. It is important to take the time to recall specific sins instead of simply asking for a blanket forgiveness for your sins in general.

Thanksgiving: This is when you thank God for what He has done. It is also a way to remind you of all of His blessings as you go along your day.

Supplication: After you've confessed your sins and are grateful to God for what He's doing in your life, you will now be in the humble state of mind to make your requests known to Him.

Keep in mind that the ACTS model simply serves as a guide to help you, not a rigid formula to follow.

WHAT WORDS DO YOU USE?

Some people feel they're supposed to use Old English to talk with God; words like *thee* and *thou*.

You can do that if you wish, but the important thing is that God wants a real, honest conversation with you, the way you might sit down and chat with someone you love and respect.

Of course, the more consistently you chat with God, the deeper your relationship will be with Him.

Do You Have to Pray Out Loud?

At the outset, praying aloud may be intimidating for some partners.

The best remedy is for one person to pray out loud, while the more reserved person sits nearby, perhaps holding hands, and listens. But don't be surprised if, after a few weeks, the reluctant person begins to emerge as a strong prayer leader, boldly *speaking* up.

SQuire
What About the Little Things?

This is a false notion that seeps into the thinking of some: that with everything God has on His plate every day—all the really big, important matters before Him—he surely doesn't have time for the "little things" concerning you.

That is simply not true.

God not only wants to hear about every detail of everything you want to talk with Him about, He will listen to you on end, for hours and hours if you want Him to. He is never "unavailable," He never takes a lunch hour, He is always there for you, around the clock and on holidays.

How do we know this?

Louise and I talk with Him all the time. You are so important to Him that "Even the very hairs of your head are all numbered," [3] "Not a single sparrow can fall to the ground without your Father knowing it," [4] and "You are more valuable to God than a whole flock of sparrows." [5]

Because "He delights in every detail" [6] of your life, you can "cast all your anxiety on him because He cares for you." [7]

Louise
CAN WE PRAY ABOUT ANYTHING?

God has absolutely no limits on what you can pray for—and don't let anyone tell you that He is "much too busy" to worry about your "petty" issues.

You are told redundantly in the Bible that you can indeed pray for anything. For instance:

> *Ask and it will be given to you;*
> *seek and you will find; knock and*
> *the door will be opened to you.*
> —MATTHEW 7:7

If anyone challenges your prayer requests, lead them to the above scripture and inquire, "Where does it say that only 'big and important' things will be given to you?"

In fact, the Bible says, "God will meet ALL your needs." [8]

God is in the details. No request is too small to place before Him.

He promises that when you trust Him and delight in Him, He will give you the desires of your heart. [9]

I find myself asking God about everything: from healing a family member to guiding me to a lost earring. And every so often, I hum a tune that reminds me:

> *And he walks with me, and he talks with me.*
> *And he tells me I am his own,*
> *And the joy we share as we tarry there . . .* [10]

Is There a Special Time to Pray?

From God's point of view, you never need a schedule; as we said above, He's on speed-dial for you, twenty-four hours a day.

But it is important for you and your praying partner to establish a consistent schedule. You may find that getting up a few minutes ahead of everybody else in the morning is the best time for the two of you to pray regularly.

Others prefer praying together just before bedtime, but whenever it is, lock it in, make it part of your daily routine; otherwise your conversation with God will become the first thing to get abandoned on days when your timetable is upset by the unexpected.

If your ritual is altered—perhaps due to travel—try to keep your prayer time consistent by praying via telephone or Skype.

You may need to improvise; if you're traveling, you may find yourselves praying on the way to the airport.

This is the aim: elevating prayer to a level of importance with other habits that you would never "forget" to do—such as grooming and daily ablutions. Or, as Tim Keller noted in the last chapter, "a nonnegotiable" daily event.

Establish an attitude that God is a very dear, close personal friend whom you would never wish to offend by ignoring Him.

Should We Have a Special Place to Pray?

You live in a world that is pulling you in so many directions it's hard to stay focused. It's a challenge to quiet your thoughts. You have a busy life, a household in which people are coming and going, kids moving erratically, schedules you're trying to maintain, and then, in this book, we are suggesting that you carve out time for the Lord and pray with a partner, for forty days straight.

Does just the idea of that commitment make you wonder, *How can I pull this off*?

A starting place is to remember what He tells you: "Be still and know that I am God." [11] Find a time and place where you can *be still* and the two of you can *speak* your prayers in peace and quiet for just five minutes. You can always extend your prayer time together, but five minutes is all we ask you set aside for The 40 Day Prayer Challenge.

Scripture says, "enter your chambers, and shut your doors behind you; hide yourselves for a little while until the fury has passed by." [12]

We have a friend who knows the importance of finding a place to be still with God. She and her husband go into a walk-in closet, shut the door, and put a sign on the doorknob that says "Prayer Time." (You're right: you need a large closet.)

If you don't have a quiet corner or sanctuary in your home, go for a walk; just you, your partner, and the Lord. As you take notice of the songbirds, the beauty of the flowers, the vastness of the sky, the prayers you speak will have a new connectivity to God and you'll feel Him calming your heart and mind.

When you and your partner allow yourselves to become still and know that God's footsteps are right there beside you, that's when you can hear God's voice. When you tune out all the cacophony of sound and listen for the voice of the shepherd, you'll know you're heading where He wants you to go. He says, "My sheep hear My voice and . . . they follow Me." [13]

As you *speak*, *believe*, and *expect* positive outcomes for your concerns, be sure to express gratitude to God, for what He is doing in your life.

How Do I Express Gratitude?

If you're not sure what words to use as you begin speaking your prayers, try just thanking God.

If you're unclear what to say next—thank Him more.

If you don't know how to finish your prayer, thank Him.

The point is, you can never overexpress your gratitude to God. You can thank Him:

- for specific favor you've received
- for guidance and instruction on difficult matters
- for the hope you feel
- for the good health of you and your family
- for all the beauty of nature all around you
- for His patience with your weaknesses
- for His mercy and kindness in helping you
- for His faithfulness—He's always there
- for His protection of you and your loved ones
- for listening and answering your prayers
- for His truth in His Word

Prayer and praise go hand in hand.

Is Praying with a Partner Better than Praying Alone?

Once you begin Partnered Prayer, you will begin to experience the phenomenon of how two people praying together is simply more powerful than one praying alone.

Partnered Prayer draws you closer to God and yields more

blessings than you could have imagined. You will find yourself helping and encouraging each other. You'll discover that it is sometimes easier to share your deepest concerns, in the presence of God, than you ever thought.

SQuire
LEARN TO CHERISH YOUR PRAYER TIME

I've fostered the habit of bringing my wife her coffee and a bagel at seven in the morning—wherever we are, I keep that routine, even on the road. It's a way for me to honor her. But it's also our established morning routine.

We have breakfast in bed. Then, around 7:15, we pray. We each pray aloud for five minutes or so, thanking God for all the favor He's shown us since yesterday, and we discuss with Him our challenges and concerns for the day.

I've called it our Daily Board Meeting. He's the Chairman of the Board. We report in.

I remember how impressed I was when I first understood the power of that scripture that says, "a cord of three strands is not quickly broken"[14]—meaning you, your partner, and God.

We view our daily gathering with God as three cords connected by clasped hands. Louise imagines that her right hand is holding God's and her left hand is in mine; my right hand holds hers as my left hand grasps God's. We feel the Holy Spirit moving among the three of us; the energy, the ideas, the solutions, the balm—it all moves through this Holy connection as we plug into the greatest power source in the universe.

Before wrapping up our prayer time with a reading from the

scriptures, which helps us to get into alignment with the source of all wisdom and knowledge that He has provided for us, we focus on our MPL—a Morning Prayer Lineup of people that we've pledged to pray for.

Our daily breakfast-in-bed prayer is one of our most cherished customs. If ever we get off-kilter—which is rare—the day just doesn't go right until we again come back together in prayer.

How Can Prayer Break Through Walls of Despair?

Almost every couple, every family, and every friendship goes through difficult seasons. Feelings of frustration and betrayal seep into the relationships and start to build walls, brick by brick. One day you get up and realize a barrier has been erected between you and the other person.

Praying together can break through any wall you thought was impenetrable. Holding hands when you pray is the first connective. As you speak the words of prayer, believing God is listening— and that He is holding your other hand—you can expect your hearts and minds will soon be melded with God's, as His healing love surges through a heavenly pipeline bonding the three of you.

Yet you and your partner may still feel you're different, and that the mountains of issues *you're* facing are so tall that you cannot imagine any way to scale them, any way to find any promise of hope, love, and peace on the other side.

In the following story, see if the matters Ceil and Al encountered were any less difficult than those that you and your partner are facing.

AL AND CEIL KASHA: BREAKING THROUGH TO THE MORNING AFTER

"I want you to leave," said Ceil through a stream of tears. She hastily packed his suitcase. "I can't stand this anymore." The very slamming of the suitcase was an exclamation point to her feelings. "Not everything's my fault!"

"I didn't say it was," observed Al, bewildered and frightened by his wife's actions.

"I need some time alone. We both do," she said. "You won't help yourself, so how can I help you?"

"Nobody can help me," he answered weakly.

Al Kasha, the composer whose Academy Award–winning song "The Morning After" promised, "There's got to be a morning after, if we can hold on through the night," had just reached his personal bottom in a cascading torrent of despair.

For months and months he had been struggling with a phobia most people can't begin to understand: the fear of leaving the house, getting into a vehicle or a plane, even the fear of seeing other people. It's called agoraphobia, and it is more immobilizing than claustrophobia.

For Al it started with heart palpitations prior to meetings and hyperventilating as he got into a car. It steadily escalated into avoiding people and travel altogether.

The fact is, it started long before with his abusive, alcoholic father.

One day in particular lurked just below the surface, in the shadows of his mind. He was eleven. He loved music and was playing Curly in a seventh-grade production of *Oklahoma!*

Arriving late, his father came down the aisle of the theater and in a loud, drunken voice asked, "Where's my Alfred?"

At home later, Al made a mistake. He said to his father, "Daddy, why did you have to talk?"

That was it. He received the worst beating of his life. With the smell of whiskey in the air, his father's huge fists slammed against both sides of his ribs, and a half-empty whiskey bottle was smashed over his head.

With blood running from his scalp, down his cheeks, and onto his lips, he felt his father roughly grabbing him and shoving him into a closet.

"How does that feel, big shot?" bellowed his father.

Pounding on the door, Al cried, "Please, Daddy, let me out." The smells of mothballs and shoe leather were suffocating.

"Big shot!"

"Daddy, please, I'll be good."

It seemed like a long time before he heard scuffling, and then a policeman was pulling him from the closet.

Despite his success, two Academy Awards for best songs, and two more nominations, Al Kasha was becoming a prisoner in his own life by this creeping malady, fearing panic in public places: agoraphobia.

Al and Ceil were to attend an opening for the musical he wrote with his partner, Joel Hirschhorn, *Seven Brides for Seven Brothers*. Ceil had made all the arrangements and for several weeks had encouraged him, notwithstanding Al's litany of objections to taking the trip. She coaxed him all the way to Los Angeles International Airport, and standing at the door, as the flight attendant collected boarding passes, he froze.

"It'll be fine, wait and see," assured Ceil, with the patience of Mother Teresa.

"I can't go."

"You've got to. Our luggage is already on. You can listen to music with the earphones or watch a movie. It'll be over in no time."[15]

Ignoring her and the attendant, Al stepped aside, as if he were grasping for something that was not there, managed to sit down, and placed his head in his hands. *Why don't they understand that getting on that plane is certain death?* he wondered.

Al and Ceil went back home that day. Their luggage took the trip without them.

Weeks later Ceil was finally at the breaking point. Arguments were constant. Al refused to leave the house for therapy. She just didn't know what to do. On top of that, it seemed to her that he was blaming her for every wrong.

This was it. "I want you to leave," she repeated.

The next three weeks were utter misery for Al. Staying at a friend's apartment, he couldn't face the world. In a sleepless state, one morning at three o'clock he was overwhelmed with hopelessness.

"I heard myself moan, and the moaning built into a gasp, then a sob, then tears poured out. My body trembled, and the tears splashed from my eyes and down my face. I tasted those bitter drops on my tongue and the crying grew wilder, more desperate."

He remembers reaching for the television dial as though it were a life preserver.

On the screen came Robert Schuller, whose *Hour of Power* program was telecast from the Crystal Cathedral in Orange County.

In a divinely aligned moment, God was about to wink. The very instant Al Kasha focused his eyes upon the pastor on TV, he heard seven words that changed his life: "God's perfect love casts out all fear."[16]

Up until that moment, Al's life had been under the control of the Enemy—all-consuming discouragement, distrust, and utter despair.

As the seven words were *spoken* by Dr. Schuller—a man who passionately *believed* what he said, having a deep faith in their source—the words became bathed in the love of Christ, and they shot like an arrow over the airwaves and into the dark recesses of Al's mind.

Yet Al struggled to remain a servant to the Enemy. He snarled sarcastically: "Fear casts out all *love* . . . is more like it."

But the light of God is superior. It can pierce through, and into, the darkest of dark places.

Al began to think, *Yes, I have been afraid, twenty-four hours a day. Afraid of everybody—Ceil, friends, business associates; I've been afraid of big spaces and small; afraid of failing, of disappointing people, of embarrassing myself.*

Again Robert Schuller's words reached his consciousness: "If you put your trust in Him, you'll find more trust than you've ever known."

Al's tears stopped. The words were now rushing through him, empowered by the Holy Spirit, lifting him up, giving him a child-like security.

He felt free!

Just like that, seven words—"God's perfect love casts out all fear"—had cast out all his fear!

He needed to tell Ceil. He needed to go home.

He hugged Ceil, told her of his experience, and felt a sense of renewal like none he could have imagined. Everything still puzzled him. He was a man of Jewish background who had been moved by the words of a Christian pastor on television. There was so much more he needed to know . . . to learn.

She was wary. He could sense Ceil was still not certain. But then, how in the world *could* she be, having endured so much? *How can I convince her I'm a new Al?* he wondered.

His mind flashed to a friend, Clark Mathias, to whom he had once confided they were having marital difficulties and that he'd been impossible with Ceil. His friend gave him powerful advice.

"Hold your wife's hand . . . ask if you can pray with her."

"Hold your wife's hand and ask if you can pray with her," spoke Clark, "then talk to God, confessing to Him, in front of your wife."

Following his friend's counsel, Al began, "Father, forgive me for being so rude to my dear wife. Though she's been angry with me, help me to express how much I love her."

Ceil saw indications that her husband was different. That caused her to venture to share with him something that had happened to her while they were apart. A mutual friend had taken her to church.

Looking at each other deeply for a long moment, they both realized God was doing something in their lives.

The next day Ceil and Al went to church together. As he sat in the pew squeezing her hand, looking around at the people and the structure, he remembered two separate conversations in the past with two different men in the film business. One was named Mark. One Gary. They both exuded joy. Both confessed they'd been through tough times. Both were Jewish. And both had said they had found joy in Jesus.

Every day for the next two weeks Al continued to invite Ceil to pray together. He did all the talking as he held her hand, feeling warmth, sensing the Holy Spirit was moving between them. Then one day, having seen her husband's heart, Ceil began to feel confident Al was a man who had now fallen in love with God, in addition to her, and she said, "Let me pray today."

Al and Ceil have been praying together ever since.

Until it had been pointed out by one of his friends, he never realized the song he and Joel had written long before he was saved—"The Morning After"—had a Christian theme to it: "There's got to be a morning after . . . it's not too late, we should be giving. Only with love can we climb. It's not too late, not while we're living." [17]

With God everything fits together with Divine Alignment.

Al and Ceil started holding Bible studies at their home that grew and grew. Eventually they merged into the Oasis Church of Los Angeles.

How Do You Measure the Effectiveness of Praying Together?

If you establish a habit of acknowledging God's role in all the good things that have happened to you since yesterday, expressing daily gratitude for His favor, you will see clear patterns of answered prayer.

It's easy to go through your daily activities, feeling good about your successes in business or accomplishments with other people, but then fail to connect the dots that God was the one who answered your prayers.

Louise
KEEPING A PRAYER LIST

We have a good technique to measure the effectiveness of our prayers at the end of every year. One of our traditions is to gather the family's prayer list to start the New Year.

Some might think of them as "goals," but writing down your aspirations for the coming year as a prayer list means you're including God in all the things you hope to do.

The most fun is to look back with amazement at our last prayer list to see how many of those requests from twelve months ago were actually answered! We are always pleasantly surprised and appreciative of the vital role God has played in getting us where we had hoped to be.

You don't need to wait until the end of the year. You can start now to establish a prayer list with your prayer partner. In a month or two you'll see a map of God's confirmations of favor in your life.

WHAT IF YOU'RE MAD AT GOD?

Perhaps you asked God to heal your health, marriage, or financial situation and you still have no evidence he has heard you.

God has not abandoned you. He loves you unconditionally.

Just because we're not able to understand the perspective of the Lord—because we're like tiny creatures at the bottom of a towering redwood tree looking up, trying to comprehend how we fit into the whole forest—we must hold on to the truth in His Word, that though we now see things "dimly," [18] someday we will see clearly and understand how God answered our prayers.

We have dear friends, Cathy and Ken Campbell, with whom we've shared laughter and tears through the years. Ken was the pastor of our little church on Martha's Vineyard. We were saddened when they told us that they were going to retire, but we also rejoiced knowing that they would have more time to spend with their grandchildren and follow their dreams to begin new ministries for the Lord. Ken was going to volunteer his services as a mentor for young pastors while studying for his long-desired doctorate. Cathy was going to encourage young women. It was going to be a new and exciting chapter in their book of memories . . . until their lives changed forever.

CATHY AND KEN'S LAST BIKE RIDE

Soon after retiring, Ken and Cathy decided to vacation in Maine, where they enjoyed the seaside, lobster dinners at sunset, and riding bikes on winding paths through the beautiful Acadia National Park. Little did they anticipate their world would be turned upside down with tragedy. In his journal, Ken wrote:

> While taking a leisurely bicycle ride, Cathy lost control, veered off the path, hit a tree and fell back onto a rock, fracturing her T5 vertebra and injuring her spinal cord.
>
> We thank the Lord that my cell phone reception was strong, despite the remote location; Park Rangers were on site within five minutes, The Bar Harbor ambulance five minutes later, and within an hour of the accident Cathy had been airlifted to the Eastern Maine Medical Center.
>
> Cathy is paralyzed below her rib cage; her internal organs are not damaged and she has full control of her upper body.

That evening Ken called to tell us what happened. We were devastated and immediately put Cathy on every prayer list we knew. We prayed diligently for a miraculous healing, which has not yet happened. Nine years later, Cathy is still paralyzed.

We must hold on to our faith and be content that God's ways are called "mysterious" for a reason: man does not have all the answers.

Still, we often marvel that Cathy and Ken have a much more positive attitude than we could imagine were we to be in the same situation. Perhaps a key to their resolve, and a godwink, is something Ken wrote: "On the morning of the accident, Cathy and I were reading the Charles Spurgeon Devotional. We were on Psalms 112:7, 'He shall not be afraid of evil tidings.'"

After the accident Cathy and Ken moved to Texas to be near family, where it would be easier to receive doctor's care and get around in her wheelchair. Ken had to discontinue his doctoral studies to become Cathy's full-time caregiver while the always sweet and cheery Cathy had to deal with constant pain in parts of her body that one would think would be devoid of feeling because she is paralyzed.

On a recent visit to their home, Cathy and I had a wonderful and enlightening heart-to-heart talk.

I asked her if she was mad at God for her situation. She smiled that light-up-a-room smile and said, "Oh no! I'm excited to see how God is going to use this."

She's an inspiration. Of all my friends, Cathy Campbell has the perfect reasons to be mad at God, to be filled with anger and resentment for what happened to her, but instead, she is looking forward, with almost childlike wonder, to see what adventure God has in mind for them.

Here's the update on their lives:

Ken returned to his studies, changed course, and was awarded a doctorate in Disability Ministries; he speaks publicly helping churches find ways to be more inclusive to people impacted by disabilities.

Cathy has become a wonderful inspirational speaker from her wheelchair, talking about God's grace and mercy even in suffering.

They recently returned from India, where they were invited to speak and pray with people at the first-ever India-wide disability conference in Delhi, touching many with the love of Christ. Says Cathy, "I can't wait to return." In fact, they were invited to return two years later.

Regardless of your life experiences, don't lose heart. Have faith that God has a purpose for everything—even your hurts. You can choose to be mad at God or you can praise Him in spite of your circumstances.

Ask Cathy's opinion about those who get mad at God, and she is likely to give you a warm smile and quote scripture: "God tells us that, 'He will never leave you, nor forsake you,'[19] and that you must never be afraid and discouraged."

> *"The LORD is good, a refuge in times of trouble.*
> *He cares for those who trust in him."*
> —NAHUM 1:7; NIV

ARE YOU INCLINED TO BE DISCOURAGED?

Jesus told his disciples that "they should always pray and not give up."[20] Paul expanded on that, warning, "Let us not become weary in doing good; for at the proper time we will reap a harvest if we don't give up."[21]

Do you believe them?

When you think your prayers are not getting answered—when your problems are so big you think nobody can fix them—do you give up on talking with God about them?

Prayer can be hard work. It requires the discipline to commit valuable time to speaking with the Lord, directly and earnestly about your concerns, and then believing He is really hearing you. That's why praying together with someone gives you immediate encouragement, providing both of you with accountability partners to keep you going and boosting the velocity and trajectory of every prayer heading up to God's attention.

> *Though one may be overpowered,*
> *two can defend themselves.*
> —ECCLESIASTES 4:12

SQuire
WILL GOD HEAR YOUR CRIES?

Yes. I know this, personally.

Six white-coated doctors and nurses moved rapidly. Their wrinkled brows and strained eyes sent me signals of alarm. If they were worried, *I* was worried.

My normal demeanor of optimism hadn't fully accepted reality—the surreal concept that I was in a hospital emergency room at three thirty in the morning having a heart attack!

"Are you worried?" I said to the doctor next to my bed.

Speaking evenly, suggesting he was more worried than he was

willing to let on, he placed another nitroglycerin tablet in my mouth and answered: "Your blood pressure is dropping dangerously low. We're trying to stop it."

The pain—not over my heart, where I thought a heart attack would be, but at the center of my chest—continued to press down. Once again the nitroglycerin had no effect. The doctors were losing options.

"I want to see my wife," I commanded abruptly; Mr. Nice Guy was now speaking like a drill sergeant at death's door!

Louise had been instructed to remain in the waiting room. She was the only one there—other than the nonchalant lady at ER reception who had refused to call a doctor until the paperwork was completed and who, if I hadn't passed out on the floor, would still be processing my credit card.

Gripped with fear and anxiety, my dear wife tried to block out the gruesome thoughts that were trying to command her attention: the awful prospects of life alone without her twenty-four-hour-every-day, inseparable soul mate.

"Would you come with me, please?"

A nurse was standing at her side.

"Your husband is asking for you."

As Louise approached my gurney, the masked doctors and nurses respectfully stepped back as if they were directed by an unseen conductor.

I looked at her, as I so often do, my eyes communicating my inner thoughts that she frequently has the amazing ability to read: *Oh, how I love you,* I silently transmitted.

She gazed at me with her tear-streaked face, unable to use words, just nodding, *Yes, I know, my darling. And I love you.*

Oh, how I wished I could erase the pain on her face and the

terrible worry I knew she was carrying. I reached toward her. She grasped my hand tightly with both of hers.

"Let's pray," I said, *speaking* firmly. "Please help me, God. Please save my life. And please, Lord, comfort my wonderful wife."

As the words left my lips, I *believed* God would rescue me. And I *expected* the favorable outcome was already done.

I don't exactly remember what happened next. Just that my gurney was being rushed down a hallway. I was lifted into an ambulance.

"What's happening?" I asked, no longer feeling the pain in my chest.

"You're stabilized; we're taking you to Norfolk Heart," said the paramedic.

I learned later that as soon as Louise and I had prayed—crying out to God—the plummeting in my blood pressure had stopped. I was sufficiently stabilized for them to transport me to nearby Norfolk Heart Hospital, one of the best in the nation.

Still, the emergency continued. Two of the veins to my heart were 100 percent blocked.

Now in another hospital waiting room Louise was again alone with her thoughts . . . the haunting thoughts of what life would be like alone should I fail to survive.

She tried to dismiss such a catastrophic tragedy, gazing around the room, thinking, *Oh, God, I wish I had my Bible.* The only thing in sight were dog-eared magazines. Then she saw it. Sitting on a chair.

Was that a godwink? Had someone left their Bible behind?

Quickly Louise lifted the volume like a treasured tome. *God, please let me know my husband will live*, she pleaded.

Her eyelids closed as she took in a deep breath, opened the Bible randomly, and then opened her eyes to discover what personal message God had just for her.

She looked down upon these words written in the book—a personal message from God about her husband:

> *When he calls out to me, I will answer him.*
> *I will be with him in his distress.*
> *I will deliver him, and I will honor him.*
> *I will satisfy him with long life."* [22]

The Holy Spirit had given her instant confirmation!

Her mind cut to the image of grasping my hands as white-coated attendants stood by, and hearing him call out to God—"Please help me, God"—and here, among 789,604 words in the scriptures, God was answering her, with a clear, encouraging, person-to-person message. She had opened the Bible to Psalms 91:15.

Tears filled her eyes as a flicker of peace passed through her.

At 8:00 a.m., I awoke. Louise was next to my bed, stroking my brow. A pleasant doctor was at my bedside, introducing himself with what seemed like an Indian accent.

"I'm Dr. Pangrahi, your heart surgeon. You are doing well."

"Dr. Pan—?" I attempted to repeat.

"Call me Dr. Pani, everyone does." He chuckled. "We inserted two stents in the two veins almost entirely blocked. You will need four other stents at a later date."

Moments later he left.

Louise and I were alone. We looked at each other. Then holding on to each other, we wept.

Only now could we process what had happened. I had been at the brink of death. With no other option available to the doctors, in total desperation, holding my wife's hand, I *spoke* out to God: "Please help me." I was saying the very words Louise would read a few minutes later as she desperately opened the Bible: "When he calls out to me, I will answer him."

Our prayers were answered immediately with the halting of the drop in blood pressure. I *spoke it*, *believed it*, and *expected it*.

And God confirmed it as Louise opened the Bible to that very comforting scripture.

Six weeks later we returned to Norfolk Heart Hospital to have the additional four stents inserted. But before entering the operating room, Dr. Pani had a puzzled look on his face as he held up the EKG, slowly moving his head back and forth.

"I am the doctor who put in the first two stents," he said to Louise and me with astonishment, "but, if I were another doctor looking at this chart . . . I would see no evidence that you ever had a heart attack."

Louise and I glanced at each other. *Thank you, God,* we both said silently.

> *Prayer pulls the rope below, and the great bell rings above in the ears of God. Some scarcely stir the bell, for they pray so languidly; others give but an occasional pluck at the rope; but he who wins with heaven is the man who grasps the rope boldly and pulls continuously, with all his might.*[23]
> —CHARLES SPURGEON

Louise
WHAT IF MY PRAYERS ARE NOT ANSWERED?

We were honored that Dr. Charles Stanley, one of the foremost theologians in the world, was staying as a guest in our home. I had so many questions to ask him over dinner, but one in particular was prominent in my mind.

"What if my prayers aren't answered?"[24]

"You must persevere," he said. "You must continue praying, regardless of whether you see immediate results or not, because the longer you intercede for a situation, or for another person, the more tightly your heart will be knitted to God."

"You must persevere."

Speaking with the tender certainly of a loving grandfather, Dr. Stanley continued, "Prayer binds us together with the Father, with a spiritual bond that lasts into eternity. Therefore, endure in your loving, compassionate, hopeful supplication for others, and always be confident that 'the effective prayer of a righteous man can accomplish much.'"[25]

When you *speak, believe,* and *expect* the beneficial outcome of your prayer, you can accomplish much. Because you serve an extraordinary God, He will make your prayers powerful.

SO, WHO'S AGAINST PRAYER?

This question is so important that we've devoted an entire chapter to it later in this book. But let us give you a sneak preview.

At this very moment there is a hidden force trying to stop you from learning about the extraordinary power of prayer! Especially Partnered Prayer.

You may not have given much acknowledgment to this force, but it's real, and it may have already been successful in keeping you from entering into regular communication with God.

That force is Satan.

Also called the Enemy.

The last thing the Enemy wants you to *know* about is the amazing qualities of prayer—a power that grows exponentially when two people come together to *speak* prayer on a regular basis.

And the last thing he wants you to *do* is to engage in consistent prayer with your spouse, family member, or friend. He doesn't like that. When you do, he'll be locked out.

But this is important: unless you give him power—the Enemy is *powerless*.

He will try to deceive you, distract you, disorient you, and discourage you, but he can't—*unless you allow* it.

When you learn to put on the "full armor of God," wearing it boldly, day in and day out, the Enemy is nothing but a puny, toothless tiger pawing the ground outside the fortress that you and your praying partner have created with God.

You are then, literally in the light, making it very hard for the Enemy to lure you into his darkness. Like a roach or a rodent, he hates the light. He runs from it.

You must always be on guard. The Enemy lies in wait expecting you to show signs of weakness. Once he sees the tiniest opening, he'll deceitfully try to lure you into a snare he's set for you, to entrap you into circumstances or addictions that will be hard to escape.

What is the Enemy's biggest enemy?

Your prayers. Especially *speaking* your prayers with a partner.

When you *speak it, believe it, and expect it*, he runs for the hills.

GET READY FOR AN AMAZING EXPERIENCE

The 40 Day Prayer Challenge is an experience that you'll never regret and never forget.

In the ten years that we have been encouraging Partnered Prayer, urging people to pair up and commit to praying five minutes a day for forty days, we have *never had a single partnership* who faithfully prayed for forty days come back to us and say, "Well, we tried it, and *nothing happened.*"

On the contrary, nearly every couple and partnership has reported that within two weeks—often within one week—they were onto a new pathway of peace and joy in their relationship. Then they were excitedly telling us amazing outcomes.

We hope you'll take the Baylor University survey at PrayStay .org—it takes no more than ten minutes—on your first and fortieth days, and get ready to open a brand-new chapter of joy and happiness in your life.

Even more significant, we expect this first empirical study to be a powerful tool for churches in changing the perception of the power of prayer to save marriages and families. You will be a part of this important work.

THE 40 DAY PRAYER CHALLENGE BEGINS NOW

This is the time, after reading these first two chapters, that we ask you to begin the Challenge.

For the integrity of the Baylor research data, each partner will take the survey separately and receive his or her own user name and password.

These two points are important:

1. In order to participate in the survey, **each person must have their own email address**.
2. **When you sign on at PrayStay.org, you and your partner must initially sign up together, on the same device;** i.e., the same smartphone, tablet, or computer. You will each create a unique login and password.

If your partner is not physically present, designate one person to sign up on behalf of both of you. That person must then pass on the unique login and password information to his/her partner, who can then change the password on their own device if they so desire.

Once you have signed up and the system knows your name, your password, and the church or organization you are associated with, you can then sign in on separate devices to take the survey, or you may take the survey on the same device, one after the other.

CHAPTER 3

PARTNERED PRAYER

Entering into Partnered Prayer is a concept that is new to many people.

As we travel the country speaking about the merits of Partnered Prayer, we never cease to be amazed by the number of people who ask "How do you do it?" or the numbers of those working in the church who privately admit that they rarely pray with their spouses or family members, except at times of crisis or for grace at dinner.

Why is this?

Mostly because the idea of two people—especially a couple or two family members praying together—never dawned on them; it's a concept nobody ever suggested. And if they did, it was an idea that seemed to run counter to their vulnerability and comfort zone.

Of course, it is not a foreign concept in the scriptures.

The idea of two people praying together is not our idea—far from it—it's suggested by Jesus in the Bible. He said, "If two of you on earth agree about anything they ask for, it will be done for them by my Father in heaven." [1]

Christ did nothing without prayer, and His directive that we should pray together is very clear.

A cord of three strands is not quickly broken.
—ECCLESIASTES 4:12

THE OBVIOUS BENEFITS OF PRAYING TOGETHER

We are prepared to claim boldly that the vast majority of people who enter into Partnered Prayer will soon be found promoting its benefits to anyone they encounter.

But in the following subsections of this chapter, rather than our telling you what people have to say, we'll let couples, family members, and friends tell you themselves about the merits of Partnered Prayer.

HOW THIS CHAPTER EVOLVES

The following three subsections address different experiences through a variety of testimonials; you can either read the section most applicable to you, or you may find that all three fit your needs:

Section A: Couples, Married and Unmarried
Section B: Families
Section C: Friends

SECTION A
COUPLES

This part is written for married and unmarried couples who are contemplating stepping into The 40 Day Prayer Challenge for as little as five minutes every day.

When you look at this experience as an opportunity to radically improve your relationship within a matter of days, or at most a week or two, we hope you'll have an attitude of wonder and excitement.

We imagine you are asking, "You mean there really is a way for the two of us to get our relationship back on the right track?" Or, if it's already going well, "to make the relationship between us absolutely sensational?"

The answer is yes. But we have to first cross a bridge: getting both partners to agree to pray together. Sometimes that bridge looks daunting.

REASONS FOR RELUCTANCE TO PRAY TOGETHER

The cause could be . . .

- You don't wish to appear vulnerable in front of your mate.
- You have secrets you don't want to come out.
- You fear your spouse or partner's expectations are too high.
- You don't have time for prayer.

THE BIG ONE: LACK OF TIME

If we were standing with you in your kitchen right now carrying on a conversation, might it unfold like this?

Q: As couples, do you pray together?
A: You don't understand, we're very busy. The demands of my job . . . my family . . . everything going on in our lives . . . at seven a.m. this place looks like Grand Central Station.
Q: Sounds familiar. Let me ask you this . . . how much time do you spend shaving or combing your hair?
A: Five minutes, probably . . .
Q: Wouldn't God love five minutes of your time?

Makes you think, doesn't it?

HOW DO I GET MY MATE TO PRAY WITH ME?

It only takes one partner to begin. Some wives—and husbands— have told us they've approached their partner this way: "Honey, will you sit with me and hold my hand while I pray for us? You don't need to say a thing, unless you want to."

As we said, starting to pray together may seem like a vast, scary, unfamiliar bridge to cross. Yet by taking that first step—holding your partner's hand and just listening—it becomes merely a footbridge. And you can't imagine the joy that awaits you on the other side.

Look what happened with this couple.

Leslie's Journey with Erick

I was so proud of my husband, Erick, on Father's Day. Tears streamed down his face as he stood before my parents and our children, pouring his heart out: "I didn't expect to live to thirty, not forty, and never to see my two grandchildren."

What an amazing journey he—and our marriage—have taken since we met in 1999.

Let me tell you my story.

I had fallen away from the church after my first marriage ended in divorce. Then Erick and I met in a bar. Not the greatest of starts.

With seven kids between us, we struggled to hold things together. I knew my husband had a drinking problem but never knew the extent of it. More and more over the next five years, he began to disappear, not coming home for long periods.

Only when his business partner confessed that Erick had been making nonstop one-hundred-dollar withdrawals from their company account did I learn I was living with a crack cocaine addict. Drugs and alcohol were robbing me of my husband and the father of our children. We lost just about everything. Our business. Our home. Friends. And it nearly cost us our marriage.

That summer my parents and I found Dr. Paul Hardy's ministry, Recovery for Life, and though Erick struggled and tried to leave during the first three or four meetings, he finally stopped drugs and alcohol. He's been sober ever since.

It was a rough start, but we began actively working a biblical twelve-step recovery program, attending church, and developing a core group of support. Step by step Erick and I rebuilt our marriage. Where mistrust and frustration had taken over, pieces were going back together, and changes were taking place in our lives, noticeable mostly to our children, whose behavior is so influenced by their parents.

We began reading the Word each day. First on our own, then reading together. But whenever I asked Erick to pray with me, he'd say, "I'm good."

I knew the power of a husband and wife praying together. As a child I had watched my dad lead our family in daily prayer. I'd seen Dad pray with Mom and knew the bond that a praying couple forms.

I just kept asking Erick, day after day.

In early 2009 we opened our home for Bible studies starting with *The Love Dare*. It's a small group study that raises the awareness of couples to do acts of kindness for each other, such as leaving hidden love notes or doing small appreciative things. It was exciting to see how our marriage improved. And, at the end of the series, we renewed our vows.

Still, we were not fully praying together. I would pray out loud and he would listen. He'd say "Amen," and that was it.

The next study our group undertook was *Couples Who Pray*, committing to pray together, five minutes a day for forty days.

One week into our routine I had made breakfast. Erick was at the kitchen table and I was reading the Bible study for the morning. I asked if he would pray with me. He replied, "How many days do I have to say, 'I'm good'?" So I just started to pray again.

Several mornings went by, and one day as I closed the Bible to start to pray, I heard my husband say:

"Dear Jesus . . ." then, silence.

I waited. I peeked with one eye to see if he was praying. I cautiously said, "Well, are you going to pray?"

I took my cue and continued the prayer. This was our new routine for two weeks.

About three weeks into The 40 Day Prayer Challenge I was sitting on the couch reading the Word. Once I closed my Bible, he said, "Dear Jesus." Again I prayed, and this time, after a long pause to see if he wanted to add anything, his only reply was, "Amen!"

I was excited. Silly as it seemed, his nonresponsiveness had moved to a "Dear Jesus" *and* an "Amen!"

By week four, my husband had moved from the kitchen table to sit beside me! And though the extent of his out-loud prayers were no more than "Dear Jesus" and "Amen!" I was overjoyed! I began to see a softening of our relationship and an increase in open communication.

Next, my husband began getting up ahead of me every morning, opening the Bible to that day's devotion. Before I came out of the bedroom, both cups of coffee were poured and we were ready to read the lesson and the Word.

Then one morning it happened!

I had been really struggling with something and, more than anything, I just wanted my husband to put his arms around me and pray *for* me, not just *with* me.

I shared my heart and my struggle, not even asking if he would pray for me, and we went on with our devotion.

When I closed the Bible, he took his cue to say "Dear Jesus." Then, he began to pray!

Tears streaming down my cheeks, I felt the burden lifting instantly. And that day was *my* day to just say, "Amen!"

I thanked him. We embraced. And I wept.

Though Erick thought it was a silly no-big-deal thing, from that day forward we prayed together! For our kids, our families, our jobs, and direction in life; together we thanked God for the many blessings, and even the chance to pray together.

Our life had been a train wreck. But God brought healing, restoration, and a peace that surpasses all understanding.

That's the power that comes when, as a couple, we pray; when we invite the Lord to be that third cord, wound tightly together, making us unbreakable. When we stand together against the things the enemy means to rob from us—our families, peace, and hope—we realize how profoundly our lives have been changed.

—LESLIE BRENNAN

Leslie and Erick were carrying a heavy load and feeling overwhelmed by their problems. Their circumstances were having a devastating effect on their marriage, children, and work. They knew they needed help.

It took courage for Erick to surrender his addiction and humble himself finally to the One who could set him free. It also took the support and prayers of Leslie, her parents, and many others. He sought recovery counseling from Dr. Hardy, someone who could guide him in his walk out of the darkness into the light. He was surrounded by family and friends who were lifting him up, praying that God would give him strength to vanquish his demons. The prayer that flowed over Erick was buttressed by the Word of Truth spoken into him.

THE WORD OF TRUTH

Many couples incorporate the memorization of verses into their prayer time so that when they come under attack they can defend themselves against the Enemy with one of the greatest weapons in their arsenal: God's Word.

When you *speak* it—God's Word—over your difficult situation, while *believing* it and *expecting* a desired outcome, the Enemy must flee.

At the end of this book you will find an appendix on prayer that you can call upon. Verses similar to this one:

> *For the Word of God is alive, active . . .*
> *sharper than any double-edged sword.*
> —HEBREWS 4:12

As you can see in Leslie and Erick's case, strongholds can be broken by combining prayer and scripture. When you weave the Word of God into your prayer, Heaven comes to attention and the Enemy releases his grip.

> *No weapon forged against you will prevail,*
> *and you will refute every tongue that accuses you.*
> —ISAIAH 54:17

WHAT'S THE BEST THING ABOUT PRAYING TOGETHER?

This is a question we love to ask couples, knowing there'll be a tone of discovery and wonderment in their voices, like they've found a gift they never expected and are surprised its contents are so overwhelming.

First, our own observations.

SQuire

To me, the best thing about praying together is *transparency*. I love never having to be on guard, hiding secret thoughts or fantasies. The three cords that bind us together in prayer—Louise, myself, and God—are like transparent umbilical cords through which the sustenance of His love and wisdom flows.

Daily prayer with my wife places a protective shield around my mind, allowing me to resist the approach of any inappropriate thought; and believe me, freedom from the shackles of secrecy is liberating!

Louise

The best thing about praying with SQuire is the intimacy I feel between each of us and God. When we pray together, I know God goes into action. He directs our thoughts and decisions. We feel His presence, His peace, and His protection.

In a relationship, prayer functions like the keel on a ship. A keel has two tasks: it prevents the boat from being blown sideways by the wind and it keeps the vessel right side up.

Praying together keeps you steady and upright. The world can pull on you and try to drag you down, but by continually connecting with God's love and direction, through Partnered Prayer, you are kept from capsizing.

When you turn to Him in prayer, seas of anxiety are calmed. He promises: "Do not be anxious about anything; but in every situation, by prayer and petition, with thanksgiving, present your requests to God."[2]

SQuire

ROSS AND LEAH: WAS THIS OUR FIRST MALFUNCTION?

We were looking forward to our lunch at the Ivy Restaurant in Santa Monica. Louise had received an email from an old friend she'd known from early days on the comedy circuit, Ross Shafer, who, through quite a godwink, I had also known from my days at ABC.

"I can't believe two of my old friends met and married," he wrote excitedly, going on to explain he too had gotten married— to a wonderful woman who was the lead praise team singer at Rick Warren's Saddleback Church in Orange County.

And here we were, barely three weeks later, having lunch with Ross and Leah, in a beautiful setting, learning about her talents and aspirations while catching up on a decade of Ross's career activities.

Louise and I prattled on about our work with Baylor University and—as we tend to do with anyone standing still—began regaling them with amazing testimonies from couples whose marriages had radically improved after taking The 40 Day Prayer Challenge.

It was a wonderful visit, and before departing, we extracted a promise from Ross and Leah to visit us if they ever got to the East Coast.

As busy people do, we went right back into a state of disconnect for the next six months. That's when Ross called and said they had a confession to make.

"Remember that lunch we had at the Ivy?" As if it were really possible we could have forgotten the delightful occasion.

"Well, we almost didn't make it to the restaurant that day.

In fact, at that time, our marriage was hanging by a thread . . . a perforated thread."

Louise and I listened with dropped jaws, recalling the picture of the perfect couple sitting across from us; we had described them later as "Ken and Barbie." Their marriage wasn't solid?

"On the drive home that day," said Ross, "I looked at Leah and said, 'Well, we've tried everything else, why not try what SQuire and Louise are talking about.'"

"I don't want to pray with you," she snapped.

"Well, I don't want to pray with you, either, but nothing we've tried has worked."

Louise and I were now like captivated attendees at a demolition derby.

"So, we tried it," said Ross, giving no indication of the outcome he was about to reveal. "For the first seven days, we prayed together . . . through gritted teeth."

I glanced at Louise, listening on another phone, our looks expressing dual concern that our first failed 40 Day Prayer Challenge was about to be unveiled.

"But, by the second week," Ross continued, "our jaws began to relax and we began to smile at each other. When we got to the fortieth day—I have to tell you—our marriage has never been better."

Louise and I literally didn't know whether to laugh or cry. I think we did both—at the same time.

Leah later told us that when they got married, their relationship was "not God-centered." She said they were both struggling with careers—hers in music, his in broadcasting—and most doors were simply not opening up.

"Then, when we began focusing on Jesus, things began to improve," she said. When they tried to have a baby they had been unsuccessful. Then, one day, without even looking for an opportunity to adopt, they were presented with a newborn baby girl.

"Lolo became the glue that helped us to stay together," Leah said, smiling.

Today Lolo is nine. She's still the glue. Not long ago she caught her parents starting to argue with each other.

"Excuse me," Lolo's little-girl voice raised above her parents'. "Have we prayed?"

It was a wonderful reminder—out of the mouths of babes— that everyone needed to stop everything, right then and there, and pray.

It works, every time.

COUPLES' FAQS ABOUT PRAYER

Following are frequently asked questions we hear from couples. Perhaps their experiences will address questions you have right now.

HOW DO WE START TO PRAY AS A COUPLE?

1. In prayer, don't try to be someone you're not, using fancy biblical terms. Just try to make it a real conversation between you, your partner, and God.
2. When you come before God in prayer, why not start by acknowledging His presence, the same way you might begin a telephone call with your earthly grandparent. Perhaps you'd say, "Good morning, Father," "Good evening, God," or simply "Hello, God, it's us."

3. Be still. God desires to be at the center of your life. So shut off the TV and silence your phone; go to a quiet place. In His Word, He advises: *Be still, and know that I am God.*[3]

4. How do you get good at praying together? Do you recall the old joke about the man walking down the street in New York? A guy asks, "How do I get to Carnegie Hall?" The man says, "Practice!"

In the same manner, you can become a virtuoso of prayer; the more you practice, the better you get, the more comfortable you feel speaking out loud to God, and the easier it becomes to know what to say when you chat with Him.

God will do amazing things when you reach out to Him in prayer. Just go ahead and try it!

Carole and Johnnie's Story

We have been married forty-five years and never prayed together.

Since starting The 40 Day Prayer Challenge, my husband, Johnnie, and I have been praying together and felt closer after only three days.

Thank you!!! This is something I have wanted for us for such a long time.

I look forward to sharing more good reports with you in the coming days.

Blessings to you, Carole.

WHAT IF OUR LIVES ARE DRIFTING AWAY FROM EACH OTHER?

Over time a wall can grow up between two people. It happens little by little, and one day you discover that you're just "going through the motions" of matrimony; you're closed off to each other and hardly recognize the person you fell in love with.

Praying together will tear down that wall, but you have to make adjustments in your life and allow yourself to be open to him or her.

Each of you needs to say, "I'm sorry, forgive me, and I love you."

Then, commit yourselves to praying together, *speaking it* faithfully for forty days. When you start out *believing* that God wants you to have an incredibly happy union and *expecting* nothing but the best relationship you know of, you're on your way to claiming it.

If you've humbled yourself and put away your pride, you soon see astonishing ways in which the Holy Spirit heals areas in your relationship that had been bothering you. God will put you on the path to drift *toward* each other, rather than apart. Before you know it—through the act of prayer—God will have melded your two hearts together, stronger than ever, becoming a fortress against anything that attempts to pull you apart.

Those wedding vows will take on a renewed meaning: "What God has joined together, let no man put asunder."

Pam and Jay's Story[4]

Almost everyone thought Jay and I had it all together.

We were at church every time the doors opened. Jay had been the children's minister at our former church, and we had good kids. It all looked good on the outside.

At home we *knew* we didn't have it together. We even mentioned getting a divorce, but we were both just too lazy. It was easier not to talk at all; when we did, it was usually disrespectful.

Jay resigned from his position, and we eventually left the church where we had raised our children. We visited Church of the Highlands near Birmingham. A few months later we were ready to join a small group and a couple of friends were leading Couples Who Pray.

I was really nervous about this because I have never prayed much—especially not out loud. It turned out to be the best thing that could have happened to our marriage. God certainly knows what He is doing when He puts people and events in your path.

Those first weeks were so awkward and strained. Jay is a better talker than me so it was easier for him, I think. As time passed we began just talking more—not about anything in particular, just talking. We began actually listening and showing some respect for each other.

Several weeks passed and we realized we were the topic of quite a few conversations about the change people could see in us; people who knew us well and those who didn't. We knew we were getting along a little better but did not realize others could notice.

Then there was a time when we were aggravated with each other—we couldn't get past it. It didn't feel like before, but we were still irritated.

I grabbed Jay's hand and prayed as best I knew how for God to remove this barrier and give us peace. When we were finished, remarkably, we both felt like a burden had been lifted and we were not at odds anymore. We felt a lightness in our hearts toward each other. I think that might be when we became the "poster children" for the group!

Do we have it all together? No.

Do we fight? Yes.

Have we come so far that we don't want to go back? Most definitely!

I believe without a doubt that God honored and blessed our tiny efforts as we began our journey and turned it into something that only He could have done.

As the weeks and months have passed we have grown in our relationship with God and each other. Only God could have restored our relationship in such a way that also grew our relationship with Him.

—Pam Jacks

When Is It Too Late to Start Praying?

It is never too late!

God has been waiting for you. He wants to communicate with His children no matter how old they are.

It is amazing how God can renew strength, faith, and joy at any age through prayer.

Barb and Kermit's Story

We've been married fifty years, finished The 40 Day Prayer Challenge, and are still praying . . . probably forty-five days now.

My husband has grown so much since the challenge began. He had only prayed aloud with me twice before in our marriage, and now we both appreciate the time together each morning.

We've grown more patient and loving with each other, and this has been the most significant growth, in a short time, that we have seen. We are just kinder with each other . . . thanks so much for that.

Gratefully,

BARB GEPHART

HOW DOES PRAYER HELP US TO LISTEN TO EACH OTHER?

When you listen to each other pray, you both hear your partner's concerns. You become more open and sensitive to your partner's hurts, fears, and desires.

Your defenses come down so you can hear with your heart, not just with your ears. Listening to your spouse in that private, safe place draws you into a more intimate relationship with God. Your focus is on helping and supporting each other.

Sometimes a commitment by you to become a better listener, every day, is just the encouragement your partner needs to reciprocate.

Kesleigh and Chad's Story

Our church had just presented The 40 Day Prayer Challenge for couples to pray together at least five minutes per day.

Well, to tell you the truth, up until this time, Chad and I have not been the most consistent prayer partners. I guess we both have just assumed that we were praying *for* each other, just not together. Which, honestly, *has* been the case.

My hubby, such a fantastic spiritual leader, instigated us taking the challenge the church had laid before us. Me, being the skeptic I am, felt like our marriage is fantastic, we don't struggle to get along . . . so what will we pray for??

After our first precious prayer together, I was *sold* that I never want to go another day without being next to my sweetheart talking to my Savior.

It's just amazing to be held by my husband, listening to him verbally thank God for the gift he was given. And what could be better than *hearing* my husband acknowledge the difficult job of mothering four kids, keeping up with a house, and trying to work outside the home? It was just precious to hear Chad ask blessings over me.

In the same way, I prayed for him in a way I've never prayed before. I was able to present specific requests for Chad and fears I know he has but doesn't talk about. It was fantastic.

I believe it will also help our parenting. It's interesting to hear the different perspectives we have regarding our children and who they are becoming. Each perspective brings a different request to the Lord. I believe our children will be blessed ten times over because of the commitment to pray together.

In a world that is ruled by material possessions, it's nice to be able to have something special that no one will ever be able to take away and that will reward us far more than anything money can buy. Thank you, Jesus, for the gift of YOU.

I'm excited to continue The 40 Day Prayer Challenge and continue to watch what the Lord does in our marriage and in our everyday lives. I strongly encourage you to take the challenge!!![5]

—KESLEIGH CASTLE

KESLEIGH AND CHAD'S POSTSCRIPT: A FAMILY CRISIS

We often talk about how learning to pray together is similar to saving money for a rainy day. In the same way as learning to save money long before your house burns down, learning to pray together puts prayers in God's bank and prepares you for unexpected days of crisis.

This is Kesleigh's note to us seven years later.

It's amazing how God works and prepares us for the future even when we can't see it. Just a few years after accepting The 40 Day Prayer Challenge, we heard the words a parent never wishes to hear: "Your child has cancer."

Instant fear, sorrow, and worry come at you full force and attack even a Christ-centered marriage and family.

Our six-year-old son Clayton endured forty-two weeks of chemotherapy, twenty-eight days of radiation, extreme sickness, and multiple hospital stays.

As a couple who had previously learned to pray together, we had the ability to pray each other through the hardest days of our lives. It was not easy! It challenged us to the core of our relationship, but our marriage — unlike so many in a family crisis — survived.

God gave us a peace that is inexplicable; the ability to be strong when we only knew how to be weak. Most importantly, He healed our son completely!

We are forever grateful for the gift of praying together and the gift of knowing that we serve a God who hears us when we cry out to Him.

— Kesleigh Castle

God's creatures are disciplined and consistent.

In the summer ants gather all of their food and save it . . .
so when winter comes there is plenty to eat.
— PROVERBS 6:8, NIV

We must do the same with our prayer life so that when trouble comes we will have a storehouse of prayer to call upon.

DOES LOVEMAKING GET BETTER WHEN WE PRAY?

Lovemaking is more than a physical act. It's also a spiritual act. God made man and woman to love and to please each other. In Romans 12:10, His Word says: "Be devoted to one another in love. Honor one another above yourselves."

We have asked many couples why they think their love life got better after they began praying together on a regular basis. Here's a sampling of the comments:

- "When the spirit and body come together as one, you can't help but have a beautiful love life!"
- "Our conversations are more meaningful as opposed to superficial."
- "Prayer time helps us eliminate feelings of resentment."
- "Praying together helps me to see into my spouse's heart and soul."

DO ARGUMENTS DECREASE WHEN WE PRAY?

"Everyone fights when they're married, don't they?" asked Meegan rhetorically. "Well, we were in a season of bickering when we took The 40 Day Prayer Challenge."

Meegan and Donald found that when they started praying together regularly, there were breakthroughs in situations that had been festering for a long time.

"We were taken aback," says Donald, with boyish excitement. "We both knew it had to do with our praying together."

"There is something about intimacy with God," added Meegan with a sense of wonder, "that lets you see the other person's heart. It makes you put down your weapons!"

The Baylor/Gallup research evaluating partners who increased their prayer time from "sometimes" to "frequently" indicated a reduction in disagreements by nearly 10 percent.

But the more impressive testimony came from the twenty-four test couples who agreed to take The 40 Day Prayer Challenge for our book *Couples Who Pray*. After the first two weeks, without exception, every couple reported a drastic reduction in arguments.

SECTION B
FAMILIES

In this section we speak to the wonderful attributes of two family members making the commitment to pray together, five minutes a day for forty days: a mother and daughter; a father and son; two siblings; or the whole family praying together.

We know the outcome prayer has when a couple prays together; the results are phenomenal, the testimonies are extraordinary.

Yet the concept works the same for any combination of family members. Arguments are likely to diminish, if not go away altogether; sharing and thoughtfulness will increase; and happiness is likely to rise.

We begin with a focus on what happens when younger children speak in prayer; later, we'll look at the outcomes of teens and older family members praying together.

Louise
DOES GOD LISTEN TO THE PRAYERS OF LITTLE KIDS?

When I was a child growing up in Quincy, Massachusetts, I never missed an episode of *The Carol Burnett Show*. I wanted to grow up to be just like her. When my friends were playing with dolls, I was in my room performing make-believe comedy routines with Carol and her costars, Tim Conway and Harvey Korman.

Growing up with a religious Italian-Catholic mother, I spent quite a bit of time at Our Lady of Good Counsel Church. As soon as we walked through the doors, my mother would drop a quarter in my hand and in her thick Boston accent say, "Heas a quata, light a candle for the souls in Purgatory!"

I would carefully drop my quarter into the coin slot, light a candle, bow my head, and fervently petition God. I figured for that price, I got but one prayer. So I'd always say: "Please, God, I just want to meet Carol Burnett!"

I felt guilty about not praying for the lost souls in Purgatory, but I REALLY wanted to meet Carol Burnett!

Every time I *spoke* it, I was certain God heard my prayer, and I had faith to believe that one day it would come true. I expected it, even though it was a tall order coming from a kid three thousand miles away from the glitz and glamour of Hollywood.

Fast-forward.

At the age of twenty I took a leap of faith and moved to LA following my dream to be a comedienne just like Carol.

I actually got myself an agent and landed some bit parts. He sent me out for an audition for a new sketch comedy TV show called *Off the Wall*. To my surprise, I got it!

It was fun to dress up and play whacky, funny characters, and I was especially thrilled when the writers handed me a sketch that spoofed Carol Burnett. I of course had studied her every gesture and vocal intonation over the years and couldn't wait to go before the cameras. Wardrobe and makeup dressed me up to look just like her, even donning me in a cropped red wig.

I was in my glory! If only for a day, it was intoxicating pretending to be my heroine.

A short while later, I was at home when the phone rang. What I heard on the other end left me speechless.

"Hi, Louise, this is Carol Burnett. [I gasped.] Listen, I saw the sketch you did of me the other night and thought it was a hoot. I would love to meet you. Why don't you come visit me next week and we'll chat."

I was floored! I pinched myself! The prayer of a little girl, from a decade before, was about to come true!

The minute I met Carol, it felt like I'd known her my whole life. I had spent hours emulating her, and now I was actually in her presence!

Carol Burnett was everything I expected: she was gracious, loving, and encouraging. It was truly one of the most memorable days of my life.

Leaving the studio I was simply astonished at how God orchestrated this—pulling off the impossible. How He did it, I'll never know in this lifetime, but I sure was grateful for it.

I looked up to Heaven and said, "Thank you, thank you . . . and oh, God . . . if I could just meet Tim and Harvey sometime . . . "

Little did I realize that by speaking those words, God would again take that request literally . . . as a prayer.

Before long, the phone rang again. This time it was Tim Conway asking if I'd like to do a touring show called Together Again, with him and Harvey Korman. I learned later that his call had nothing to do with the godwink with Carol—somehow Tim just came across one of my audition reels.

Wow, God, you're amazing!

Subsequent to that phone call, I toured with my heroes Tim and Harvey for fifteen years. And prior to every performance, I thanked God for His gracious favor, divinely aligning a little girl with a long ago prayer and a dream.

How about you? Do you remember asking if God was real? In childhood, or perhaps even today?

Tim did.

Tim Conway: Proof That God Is Real

When I was twelve years old, everyone said there was a God—I had no reason to disbelieve them—but inside I always wondered, *Really, how could anyone know for sure that God is up there listening to me?*[6]

In our little storybook town of Chagrin Falls, Ohio, the number one best day of the year was Blossom Festival. I'd get up early, look down by the river, and see that a fantasy village had sprung up overnight—a carnival, with a giant Ferris wheel right in the middle!

I was nearly breathless running down the hill one Saturday morning with five dimes shaking in my pocket. I inhaled the aromas. The smell of hot buttered popcorn blending with the pungent odor of axle grease.

Surveying my options with awe and wonder, I quickly bought a cotton candy, a Coke, and still had three dimes left to spend.

Then I saw it—hanging in a game booth—a cross on a green ribbon that glowed in the dark. Something inside demanded that I have that cross! All I had to do was to fish one particular duck from the sixty or so that were bobbing on the big tub of water.

With the tip of my tongue firmly placed in the corner of my mouth, I held the fishing pole with the concentration of a major league pitcher. But one dime after another went into the outstretched palm of the attendant. I tried and lost.

Head down, slumping toward home, I pictured how that prize would have looked in my bedroom. Oh, how I wished I could have had that cross on a green ribbon that glowed in the dark.

Then my eye was drawn to a glint of light at the edge of the sidewalk. Leaning down, I picked up a shiny dime. And, picturing myself like a guy in a slow-motion movie, I dashed back down to the carnival, filled with hope!

Anxiously, I was about to drop the dime into the outstretched palm of the attendant when the big question reemerged in my mind: *Is anybody really listening up there?*

I stopped. Walked to a nearby maple tree, leaned my head on my forearm, and said, "God, if you are really listening to me, I would like that green cross on a ribbon that glows in the dark."

Walking back to the fairway, I felt strangely more upright. I confidently placed the dime in the man's palm. Steadied the fishing pole. And I got it!

It was one of the most amazing things that ever happened to me! I kept that cross under my pillow all through college—I still have it!

—Tim Conway

Evidence that *yes*, God *is* up there listening to him was a powerful lesson in the life of Tim Conway. An experience at the age of twelve bolstered his faith for a lifetime. From a small town in Ohio to international fame as a comedic icon on television's *Carol Burnett Show*, if Tim Conway ever doubted God, he could always take himself back to the boy who leaned against a tree praying for something his heart desired; and, then, through divine intervention—a godwink—his prayer was answered. He *spoke* it, *believed* it, and *expected* it!

As children, we have a simple faith. We believe what our parents tell us as fact. Only as we grow older do we question everything.

Yet to be truly effective in prayer it is necessary to come before God with the faith of a child.

While teaching his disciples, Jesus called a child to him and said, "Unless you change and become like little children, you will never enter the kingdom of heaven."[7]

Even at eighty years of age, Tim Conway has never lost his childlike qualities. Nor his childlike faith. Knowing he still has that cross with the green ribbon that glows in the dark reaffirms the day long ago when he called out to God and God answered him.

Aren't we all children inside? With the needs of a child? For protection and encouragement?

You will always be one of God's favorite children. He wants to reaffirm to you, through your communication of prayer, that He really is up there listening to you.

Having established that God indeed hears the prayers of younger kids, let's focus on how you can get your children praying.

PRAY TOGETHER, STAY TOGETHER

"The family that prays together, stays together!" was a slogan no one could forget.

That's how Father Patrick Peyton signed off his programs in the early years of television. The catchphrase got picked up and repeated in bulletins, newsletters, sermons, and on the marquees outside of churches. And it was reiterated by parents and grandparents in the nation's households daily.

Today that slogan is the name we have adopted for the non-profit 501(c)(3) that is spearheading the drive across the nation to instigate Partnered Prayer through The 40 Day Prayer Challenge.

We know there is enormous wisdom in the words "The family that prays together stays together," as well as an inherent promise all can accept as truth.

Yet, sadly, how many families do you know who follow Father Peyton's counsel to pray together?

Can you imagine what would happen if everyone did?

SQuire
PRAYING WITH YOUNGER CHILDREN

If many of us were never taught how to pray, it is not at all surprising that we've done little to teach our children to pray.

Many parents of my generation, thinking they were doing the right thing, introduced their children to a prayer that scared them half to death. Passed down from generation to generation, it was the nursery rhyme made famous by Benjamin Franklin's publication *The New England Primer*:

> *Now I lay me down to sleep*
> *I pray the Lord my soul to keep.*
> *If I should die before I wake,*
> *I pray the Lord my soul to take.*

Yikes!

As a child I remember staring at the ceiling wondering if I'd be alive in the morning.

My dear mother, doing the best she could, tutored me to accompany the "now I lay me down to sleep" prayer with a list of those for whom I should ask God to bless. So I would kneel at the bed and redundantly say, "God bless" before each member of the family, ending with my dog, and wondering if it was appropriate to mention myself.

But generally speaking, my recitation of a handed-down poem and the list of "God blesses" were rote, not a meaningful *conversation* with God.

So how can you lead your child to God?

HERE ARE SOME TIPS

- **Children learn by example**.

  If you pray *with* your child, he or she will learn to pray on their own. Imagine the benefit when your child is faced with an issue at school and can instantly turn to God to quiet their inner worries or to help them focus on the tasks ahead of them.

- **Listen to your child's prayers**.

  Prayer, like no other communication, consistently and candidly expresses our innermost concerns—what frightens us, makes us feel guilty, or reveals the desires of our hearts. Same is true for children. Therefore, teaching your child to place all of his concerns before God, then listening to their prayers, will provide you with a deeper insight into the matters on their mind.

- **Talk with your child about worrisome matters.**

  Your youngster's prayers provide a perfect opportunity to

talk about nettlesome issues, as well as give you the chance to reestablish how their daily relationship with God will help them put on their armor for the day.

PRAYING WITH OLDER CHILDREN

As children become adolescents, they need prayer as much as the little ones; maybe more.

The world is in such turmoil. Families are being destroyed by drugs, alcohol, and pornography. Our children are being seduced into that culture. More and more of our teens reflect a self-centered world where material things mean everything and "It's all about me."

Learning from their parents, kids usually mirror their role models.

Think of the extra power you can give your offspring by bringing them up with the values taught in the Bible. It's their armor when they go into the world on their own.

If you don't pray with them, the world will prey upon them.

> *Train up a child in the way he should go,*
> *Even when he is old he will not depart from it.*
> —PROVERBS 22:6, ESV

Children who learn to pray early in their lives can be fortified against forces outside the family, as well as disappointments within the family.

The following story exemplifies how young Shelby coped with those issues.

SHELBY MEKSTO: THE PERSISTENT PRAYERS OF AN EARNEST CHILD

Eight-year-old Shelby Meksto repeated one prayer every day:

"Dear God, I just want a pet bird."

She says it all started while watching a program about different birds on the Animal Planet channel, and "from then on, my heart was just set on getting one."

Shelby's parents were not persuaded. They told her she needed to be a little older to accept that kind of responsibility. "Besides," said Sheri and Tom Meksto in unison, "we don't need another pet in the house."

They already had two dogs.

Undaunted, Shelby delved into research. She went online, checked out books from the library, and settled on an Australian cockatiel as the ideal bird to have. With a PowerPoint presentation of photos, she made her pitch to her parents.

"A cockatiel is perfect because they are small, they don't take up too much room, and are not as loud," said the young sales presenter.

As a radio sales manager, her dad was impressed. "She explained to us exactly how to take care of it and that the cockatiel has a small beak, so if they bite, they won't hurt."

Shelby persevered in her campaign to get a bird. Unsuccessful in persuading her parents, she took her presentation to God.

"During 'pray time' at my private school, my number one prayer was to ask God for a cockatiel."

At home, during grace at dinner, she always beseeched God silently—and occasionally out loud—"Don't forget my bird, God."

Eighteen months passed. Shelby's parents approached her with a difficult conversation; their dog Carona was getting old, having trouble walking, and was going to die soon.

Shelby didn't understand why God couldn't just keep her dog alive. She began to cry.

As if the cries of a little girl melted the heart of God, the most amazing godwink followed shortly thereafter. A neighbor, whom they hardly knew, telephoned Tom. He said he was doing some yard work and saw a bird in a tree. When he whistled, the bird flew to his shoulder.

"I can't keep this bird, but I know you have daughters," said the man. "Would one of them want it?"

Momentarily bewildered, Tom asked, "What kind is it?"

"A cockatiel."

"A cockatiel??"

"Yes."

Amazed, Tom said, "I have a daughter who would *really* like to come over and see that bird."

As Shelby returned home from the neighbor's she was filled with excitement. "She's the very color I wanted," she prattled, "gray with peachy cheeks. She has a Mohawk. And I know it's a girl because she has speckles under her feathers."

At last. Her parents' hearts also melted. "It was too much of a godwink and she was just too cute," said Tom and Sheri. "We had to let her have it."

The Meksto household took on an air of excitement as everyone put their full attention on the newest family member. Shelby drew upon her extensive research to tutor everyone about the characteristics of cockatiels.

A few days later the household turned sad. Carona's health failed further and she slipped into permanent sleep. Shelby cried. Carona had been part of the family all of her life.

Her dad tried to reason with her with fatherly kindness. "When one door closes, God opens another."

Shelby didn't like that reasoning.

"Why can't we have two doors open?" she protested.

Then Shelby began to recover her composure . . . and to count up her blessings. She began to see how God had really been listening to her daily prayer for eighteen months but perhaps needed the time to put all the pieces of the puzzle together. She again opened her eyes to the extraordinary godwink and was again astonished.

"Wow, this bird just flew down from heaven, right into my life," she says, "I could see how my dad was right: God closes one door and opens another!"

Shelby announced to her parents that she now had a better understanding of how God works things out. And that she had a name for her new pet cockatiel.

"Her name is Kiwi," she said with a sweet giggle, "like the Australian fruit."

PRAYING WITH GROWN CHILDREN

Do you feel that time and circumstances robbed you of the opportunity to pray with your kids when they were young . . . or in their teens?

Here's the good news. You can make up for lost time, bridging the present and the past in a most gratifying way: take The 40 Day Prayer Challenge with your adult child.

Many have gleefully reported their experiences of child-parent commitments to pray together.

Equally enthusiastic are the outcomes for fathers and daughters or sons who pledge to pray for five minutes a day for forty days.

Robert and Tim's Outcome

Due to our busy schedules and geographic separation, my son and I held our "daily board meeting with God" via telephone.

We learned it was paramount to arrange our prayer call at exactly the same time every day for forty days and to keep them short.

And here's the best news: get ready for extra-special outcomes in your relationship for years to come . . . long after your forty days are over!

—ROBERT BRAWLING[8]

PAULETTA WASHINGTON: CREATING A FAMILY CULTURE TO PRAY TOGETHER

When the voice on the other end of the phone identified herself as Pauletta Washington—Mrs. Denzel Washington—we felt a surge of excitement to receive the call.

She said she'd heard about our book and wanted to do anything she could to help support the concept of couples and families praying together.

A lunch date was arranged, and Pauletta shared how she was raised in a home where her parents always prayed with the children, and that it was a common sight for the kids to see their parents sitting quietly, holding hands, and praying with each other.

Pauletta has carried that cherished childhood memory into her marriage with one of Hollywood's most accomplished leading men. For nearly three decades, prayer has played a central role in the raising of their children.[9]

To know that every time you are facing stressful and worrisome issues, you can find comfort in the snapshot of your parents praying together is a priceless treasure to pass along to your children.

Here's another uplifting story of a family who has been weaving the principles of *speaking*, *believing*, and *expecting* into every aspect of their marriage for more than thirty years. It began with Jim and Karen praying as a couple, then extended to their two sons.

Jim and Karen's Family Prayer Journey

We are excited to tell you about our journey of praying together as a couple for the past 11,322 days; or *exactly* thirty-one years ago *today*, March 3, 2015. (How's that for a godwink?)

How did our incredible marriage begin?

It started with an intense set of external circumstances, just after our honeymoon, that forced us to get on our knees in front of our living room couch, which became our "prayer couch" for decades to come.

Praying together soon became the foundation of our marriage, and our job as parents.

We have not stopped praying and never will. In fact, our family motto is Never Give Up, Never Surrender to the issues facing us.

In addition to praying together as a couple, we have also prayed with and for our children every day, starting before they were born. We prayed over their cribs, as infants. As they got older, our nightly ritual was to kneel by their beds and pray together as a family. For many years we recited, nightly, the 23rd Psalm.

Our attitude was that the only way to teach our kids *how* to pray was to do it with them. We never said "You *have* to pray," we just prayed *with* them every day.

In the evolution of the Covell nightly prayer times, we chose to make it fun and interactive for our two boys. We wanted prayer to be lighthearted, engaging, and sometimes even silly; for them to learn that talking to God is not only important, and often serious, but fun!

Sometimes we prayed only three to five words each, creating the challenge to choose three words that represented the three most important prayer needs of that day, without wasting additional words of description.

Amazingly, we all knew what the other was asking in prayer in just three to five words. Of course, God knew about all the details!

Sometimes the four of us would *speak* a "round-robin" prayer. Each person would contribute just one word until the prayer was finished. The net effect was that we were writing the prayer together but never knowing where it was going. It was always beautiful!

On other occasions we would have a time of just listening silently to God or taking turns to pray for one another.

Who got to start depended on whether it was an even or an odd day. That way, no one argued about who started.

We had the "No Agenda Praying Rule," meaning that no one was allowed to complain about another family member's prayer, nor suggest to God that another person needed to change! At times that rule came in handy.

We had fun with grace at dinner, as well. Often we would say the Lord's Prayer uniquely, inserting the main course of that night's dinner into the line, "Give us this day our daily bread."

The result was, "Give us this day our daily pasta . . ." or "chicken" or "tacos."

Every day before our two boys got out of the car to go to school we would pray with them. We asked blessing of their day, for their teachers and friends.

Often we would gather other parents and walk the perimeter of the school and pray for the teachers, principal, and students.

We adhere to the belief that though the Supreme Court stripped prayer from our public schools, as long as there are final exams, there will *always* be prayer in schools!

Our boys have now left the nest. Our oldest is out of college, and our youngest is still attending college. But when we're together, we still pray as a family, for our needs, our joys, other family members, and friends. This cherished practice, we know and trust, will last through the end of our days together.

As a couple, we continue to pray every day, praising God and asking for wisdom, guidance, and direction. We also pray together every night before going to sleep.

To help keep our nightly prayers fresh, avoiding their becoming rote, we've developed a pattern of switching off; one of us prays for the boys with the other praying for family members and friends.

Together, we have prayed through unemployment, broken family relationships, poor health, breakthroughs, and even our son's brain tumor. God has been faithful all along.

We pray because we can't live without it. We bring God into everything we do and everything we are. We live by the quote,

"Prayer is not preparation for the greater work; prayer *is* the greater work."

Our evidence is an amazing marriage and two wonderful boys. We truly believe it's because of our lifelong commitment to prayer.

This we know: with God everything is possible; if we did everything on our own, we would just mess it up!

—JIM AND KAREN COVELL

The biblical counsel to "train up a child in the way he should go, and even when he is old he will not depart from it" [10] is sage advice. Jim and Karen Covell can rest assured that by making prayer a part of their boys' everyday life, they have given them sharp weapons to take into the world.

Their prayer together also instigated an amazing organization, the Hollywood Prayer Network, which was started as a ministry to pray for people who are working in the film and television industry—hopefully bringing many of them into a walk with God.

Fifteen years later, HPN has tabulated that there are more than ten thousand Christians working in the industry. And at this writing there are ninety local chapters of Hollywood Prayer Network in thirty countries.

Karen Covell, who serves as executive director of HPN, says she is most excited to witness a great new uprising among young people who are seeking Jesus and are now overflowing the many new churches aimed at them.

Again and again, parents like Jim and Karen Covell will joyfully testify that prayer in the family has been at the center of not only family happiness, but in guiding their entire lives.

As a child, Marian Chadwick also learned that prayer was the key to everything, and she was schooled in verses of scripture until they became second nature to her.

MARIAN CHADWICK'S BIBLE PROTECTION:
TRAIN UP A CHILD IN THE WAYS OF THE LORD

"You've got to teach your children to experience the power of God in their lives,"[11] said Marian Chadwick, the owner of a boutique store in Frisco, Texas.

That's her explanation for how she bravely caused a hooded armed robber who was holding her at gunpoint to back down and leave her store.

"Our parents taught us that you don't do anything in your life without going to God first; that there's power in prayer and in the name of Jesus."[12]

She got to test that power in a big way when the hooded man came into her little boutique store while she was waiting on a customer. She looked up and was staring at a gun pointed right at her.

"This is a robbery. I want your money," said the man gruffly, noticing she didn't wince. "Lady, I'm serious."

Marian later said that her "DNA went into immediate action as the power of God rose up" in her. She pointed her finger at the man and said, "In the name of Jesus, you get out of my store. I bind you by the power of the Holy Spirit!"

The gunman took a step back and turned to Marian's customer, ordering her to drop to the floor.

"She will NOT do that," charged Marian, again ordering him to leave the store.

She said she wasn't scared because she knew "Satan was in that man," but, quoting scripture, "that I had power in me that was greater than in him."

The man backed up and left.

"The core message of what happened was that I was raised in a way that I did not depart from the teachings of my parents and the things I knew in my spirit."

The postscript to the story is that the man was captured by police and later said in an interview that getting caught was probably a "God thing."

Marian will never forget the day she received supernatural gifts directly from God and confirmation of His Word: "You will receive power when the Holy Spirit comes on you." [13]

> You will receive power when the Holy Spirit comes on you.
> —Acts 1:8, NIV

SECTION C
FRIENDS

Choosing a prayer partner—a trusted friend with the same understanding of faith—can help you through the most difficult times and provide you with someone to share your most joyful moments.

We all sail into life's storms. But navigating the rough seas all by yourself is more difficult. With a prayer partner to help you bail out of depression and discouragement, and raise the sails of faith, you'll be blessed with God's wind at your back and be able to overcome the most painful of times.

Your partner helps you cope with every tear and every fear. Yet your deepening faith and friendship will bring into focus the joy God shines into your life every day, wonderful kindnesses that might escape your attention were you to face each day alone.

When we learned that Dee Teague and Gloria Fischer had a prayer partnership spanning many years, we asked if they'd be willing to share their personal prayer journals to give us a snapshot into the prayer life that brought them through struggles and triumphs.

We wondered how they *spoke* prayer, *believed* it, and *expected* its outcome.

We are grateful they consented. From these two special ladies we see, without a shadow of a doubt, that prayer works!

GLORIA AND DEE: THE LIFELINE OF FRIENDS WHO PRAY

Gloria's Journal

My husband was gone. After a one-year battle with bladder cancer, he took his last breath and went home to be with the Lord. I now faced life without him. I had choices to make. Was I going to focus on what I had lost or was I going to be grateful for what I had? I had many things to be grateful for: health, a beautiful home, awesome siblings, and one of my biggest blessings, my prayer partner, Dee.

Dee:

Gloria has always seemed so strong in her faith; she both challenged and encouraged me as we prayed together.

Gloria's Journal

We prayed together regularly through Allan's illness and many other life issues. It was a lifeline. Since my family is not close by, she's my local sister.

Dee:

She seemed to really need to connect each morning to pray and praise the Lord together. Before this we prayed weekly unless there was something urgent.

Gloria's Journal

We have both learned to praise God in *all* things. We never asked, "Why us?" We knew God was in control, He had a plan, and He would see us through. Instead, we asked, "What do You want us to learn?" and "How do You want to use us through this process?"

Allan had no life insurance, so I was left with debt and no way to pay it. I had not worked a job in several years. I had a small income from a business we had started but not enough to pay the mortgage and other expenses of life. So Dee and I prayed that God would provide for me.

Dee:

As we prayed, praised and trusted God to provide, I was privileged to have a front-row seat to watch how faithfully He did provide. My faith grew as I watched the amazing ways He met Gloria's every need, exceeding what we could ask for.

Gloria's Journal

I keep a prayer journal. So I began to keep track of the many ways God faithfully provided. This is just part of the list:

- One of my business partners paid $2,400 toward Allan's funeral expenses.
- My brother came from California for a week to help me with some construction projects.
- My church family quietly raised $2,500, and the deacon's team paid to have my oil tank filled.
- I got a mortgage modification so I could stay in my home.
- When I needed a new car, we prayed that God would direct me to someone I could trust. He did.
- God blessed my business in ways I could not imagine, providing thousands of dollars.

One day Dee emailed me and said the company she works for had an opening and thought I would be a perfect fit.

Dee:

I so wanted another believer to work with me, and we had prayed occasionally that God would open the way. When the job description came out, I knew Gloria was the perfect person for the job.

Gloria's Journal

I interviewed for the job and was given an offer too good to pass up. I am able to work from home three days a week, which is a huge blessing I wasn't even asking for!

Dee:

I was so excited when God answered "yes." What a blessing it is to work together.

Gloria's Journal

When I was hired, I was told there would be no bonuses that year and we would not get a raise because funds were down. We work for a nonprofit organization. God blessed them and we got both a bonus *and* a raise. God provided, and I have paid off all my debt. We are blessed to have each other. We encourage others to get a prayer partner, saying it will bless you in ways you cannot imagine.

—Gloria Fischer

Dee's Journal

My prayer partner Gloria and I pray each morning, "This is the day the Lord has made, let us be glad and rejoice in it." I was feeling joyful that this surgery on my right foot was six weeks behind me, no longer painful, and I was on my way to recovery.

I still couldn't drive, so I was going to cancel my routine mammogram for that afternoon when a friend called to invite me to take a drive and have lunch. I told her I'd love to and was going to skip my doctor's appointment anyway. She was adamant that she would take me, then we'd have a bite to eat.

Five days later I received the dreaded call from the doctor: "Mrs. Teague, you have breast cancer." I knew I needed to pray with someone, and my prayer partner Gloria was at work. A dear friend from church answered on the first ring. She'd already gone through breast cancer and survived, and her reassurance told me it would be okay.

Later, I was able to reach Gloria.

Gloria

When Dee called to tell me the news, we prayed for wisdom prior to meeting with the surgeon.

Dee's Journal

The next few weeks were a blur. They couldn't operate until the cast came off my foot. I went into a walking boot and had the surgery with all of its complications.

Gloria

During the surgery they found cancer in the primary lymph node, so they had to remove all the nodes for that arm. The drain was not placed properly, so Dee had a lot of pain. We prayed, and I could see Dee's faith growing through this trying process. She became stronger in surrendering everything to Jesus.

Dee's Journal

I could feel the prayers of Gloria and other prayer warriors uplift me. One day there were complications with getting the IV into my veins.

Gloria

We prayed for serenity. The prayer warriors laid hands on Dee's hand and from nowhere a seasoned nurse materialized and found the vein. Yeah, God!

Dee's Journal

As Gloria and I were praying I felt as if the Lord was telling me that cancer is not a disease, but a ministry. I have learned in Philippians 4:6-7, "Do not be anxious for anything, but in everything by prayer and petition, *with* thanksgiving, present your requests to God, and the peace that surpasses all under-standing will guard your heart in Christ Jesus."

Gloria and I began to thank God for my breast cancer so that He would use it for His Glory.

There are so many miracles that happened as I walked through those days of surgery, chemo, radiation, and a bout of shingles that had me in total awe of His presence. Without a tangible Lord in my life through daily reading, prayer warriors, and my sweet Gloria by my side, I know that I would have fallen apart. Through this I was given a choice of fear or faith. I chose to walk by faith through the fire.

Gloria

Dee has had many struggles and much pain, but God has been with her every step of the way. One of her requests was that she would not get mouth sores, a common side effect of chemo. We prayed and she did not. How good is our God?

Dee's Journal

They found another lump in my breast. They did a biopsy. We praised God with confidence that He knows what is best, and prayed for His will.

Gloria

Dee is really growing through this process. She is relying more on God. When she starts to slip into worry and fear, she runs to Him.

Dee's Journal

Results of the biopsy—NO CANCER! Praise God!

It is my wish for those who read this—who may be going through your own furnace of fire—that you will find someone with a deep faith and knowledge of God's Word to travel with you. Your journey to your final destiny will be so much more joyful.

—Dee Teague

"...*given a choice of fear or faith. I chose ... faith.*"

Even in the toughest of times, Dee and Gloria understood that while we can't always control what happens to us, we can control how we choose to respond. As Dee said, "I was given a choice of fear or faith. I chose to walk by faith through the fire."

They pushed through the sorrow, the sickness, and the financial stress, by thanking God in all situations. Their struggles actually made them stronger.

Be strong and courageous. Do not be afraid . . .
the Lord your God goes with you;
He will never leave you nor forsake you.
—DEUTERONOMY 31:6

THE BLESSINGS OF A PRAYER PARTNERSHIP

It's a blessing to pray with a friend. When you make the commitment to pray together for forty days you *will* see results, both in the richness of your friendship and in your walk with God. Here are some of the outcomes you can expect:

- Praying together will remove the feelings of aloneness.
- You will encourage each other.
- You will be accountable to each other.
- You will both become stronger in the Lord.
- You will cover each other in God's love and protection.
- You will have a stronger force against the Enemy.

We are called the "Body of Christ." When part of the body is hurting, the others will lift us up.

We all need the strength that exceeds our own power, and that only comes from praying with another.

The ancient scriptures are never wrong:
Two are better than one . . .
For if they fall, one will lift up his fellow.
But woe to him who is alone when he falls
and has not another to lift him up!
—ECCLESIASTES 4:9–10, NIV

THE PRINCIPLES OF FAITH

If you were to look at air, you wouldn't see it.

But you know it's there. You know the thing you cannot see is there, because if it wasn't you couldn't breathe, and you wouldn't exist.

Similarly, faith is something you can't see, but through it, you can expect the existence of things, specifically things you have prayed for.

The King James Bible spells it out:

> *Faith is the substance of things hoped for,*
> *the evidence of things not seen.*[14]

In the more contemporary language of The Word, it says:

> *Faith assures us of things we expect,*
> *and convinces us of the existence*
> *of things we cannot see.*

Thus, when we talk in this book about *speaking* a prayer, *believing* that God will answer that prayer, and *expecting* the outcome we ask for, we are exemplifying faith.

There are many biblical promises about faith. We are told that God "calls into existence things that don't yet exist."[15]

You should "live by faith, not by sight."[16]

You can protect yourself if you "take up the shield of faith with which you can extinguish all the flaming arrows of the evil one."[17]

Applying these promises to your daily life, with prayer and faith, you can ask God to call into existence money that you don't have; you can live by faith that your marriage will improve, even though improvements are not visible; you can face a negative medical report with the shield of faith, *expecting* that all the flaming arrows of the Enemy will fall helplessly to the ground, and that you will be healed.

TEN WAYS TO STRENGTHEN YOUR FAITH

1. **A prayer partner builds your faith.** Your daily prayer together will help you encourage each other to keep holding on to God's promises.

2. **Faith is like a muscle;** you need to put it to constant use in order to strengthen it. When you *speak, believe,* and *expect* your prayers are already answered, God is working on your behalf even though you see no evidence of it.

3. **Learn to wait on the Lord,** yielding to Him when things are looking bleak, and all the while trust and believe that He is divinely aligning the pieces of the puzzle that will bring you solution and peace.

4. **Develop patience** through your suffering; "waiting without murmuring or discontent" [18] as you rely on God to express His will.

5. **Be still.** Your faith develops when you're in a place where the only thing you can do is to "be still and know that I am God." [19]

6. **Acknowledge your trials as faith builders.** Where you and I see stress, God sees opportunities. He uses every crisis to draw us closer to Him. It's during those times that He can teach us many lessons. He never said we wouldn't experience

troubled waters, but He promised He would be with us as we ride out the storm.

7. **Learn to surrender all to God.** The problems we face will either overwhelm us or make us stronger and better. He wants the latter by your turning everything over to Him.

8. **Praise and worship God,** for He "takes pleasure"[20] when you praise Him for your blessings. The more you *speak* with God to express gratitude for your family, the roof over your head, or your job, the more you'll come to realize the many gifts He has already bestowed upon you.

9. **Giving testimony enhances faith.** The word *testimony* has a root in Hebrew that means "do it again."[21] When you speak and share a testimony, you are remembering what God has done for you in the past and *that* fosters faith that He will do it again. Before facing Goliath, David gave testimony to Saul that God had rescued him "from the paw of the lion and . . . the bear."[22] This gave David faith that God would again rescue him from Goliath.

10. **Learn to be salt and light in the world.** This happens by striving to emulate the gentle but principled demeanor of Christ. When you approach difficult times by faith, not by feelings, you'll find yourself more peaceful and thoughtful; people will detect God's light reflecting from you.

Therefore, confess your sins to one another
and pray for one another, that you may be
healed. The prayer of a righteous person
has great power.
—JAMES 5:16, ESV

CHAPTER 4

CHURCHES THAT PRAY TOGETHER

SMALL ARMIES STORMING THE GATES OF HEAVEN

We so admire church families that rally around their own, sometimes even reaching out beyond their own borders to assist the wounded or lost from neighboring churches.

When a family's home and worldly possessions burn to the ground, it's the churches who band together to help.

When a tornado rips through a town, it's the churches who are the first to pitch in.

When a hurricane like Katrina wipes out great sections of a state, it's the churches who are the first on the scene, feeding and clothing the displaced.

In this chapter we focus on the amazing stories of four church communities that pulled together at a time of crisis and rallied around those in need.

JIM CYMBALA: WHAT A CRAZY IDEA

This made no sense! How could a guy with no theological degree, no experience, no skills in public speaking, take charge of a rundown church in Brooklyn?

Jim Cymbala forlornly looked upon a handful of people scattered around the small, dingy, paint-peeling sanctuary. He had to stop himself from breaking down in tears or bolting.

C-r-r-a-a-c-k![1]

Adding emphasis to his misery, the front pew split in two, unceremoniously dumping five people to the floor. Jim's countenance turned to shock.

His wife, Carol, tried to cover the situation with a hymn on the organ as gasping, groaning people managed to get up and move to another pew.

So began Jim Cymbala's career as a preacher!

It started with his father-in-law, a well-respected man of the cloth and overseer of several New York area churches, who saw something in Jim he didn't see in himself. He asked Jim to take over the dilapidated Brooklyn Tabernacle Church.

Ignoring Jim's protests that he was not qualified for such a task, Rev. Clair Hutchins quietly responded, "Don't be afraid, Jim. When God calls someone, that's all you really need."

Now, here he was, feeling powerless with no sense of control over events. He muddled through the service and later sat in the pastor's office looking at the morning's offering: $85. Along with the little they had in the bank, they'd have $160. The overdue mortgage was $232. Now what?

The next day, Monday, he prayed and prayed. "Lord, you have to help me. I don't know much, but I do know we have to pay the mortgage."

On Tuesday Jim came to the church hoping that something in the mail would bring him a solution. But there was nothing, just more bills.

Crying out as he placed his head into his arms on the little desk, "God, how are we going to get through this?" For an hour he called out to God. Eventually, drying his tears, a thought popped into his mind. Besides the mail slot on the front door, the church also had a post office box.

He walked quickly down the street and opened the box. There was nothing.

Trudging wearily back to the two-story church building on Atlantic Avenue, Jim reentered the building.

There on the floor of the foyer was something that wasn't there five minutes earlier. It was an envelope. Jim curiously opened it.

Inside were two $50 bills.[2]

Jim began shouting all by himself in the empty church. "God, you came through! You came through!" He had enough for the mortgage, and even some for utilities.

For Jim Cymbala, that was the first mighty lesson for a disheartened young pastor.

Prayer works!

Still, the task ahead was daunting. As he struggled from week to week, Jim's gloom engulfed him. There seemed to be no relief from the helplessness he felt. On top of that, he suspected the usher was pilfering from the collection plate.

One Sunday, five minutes into his sermon, Jim began choking on his words. Tears filled his eyes. He looked at his small congregation and said, "I'm sorry. I can't go on."

Looking at his wife, he said, "Carol, can you play something on the piano? And would the rest of you come around this altar? If God doesn't help us, I don't know what we'll do . . ."

People came around him. As Jim again lowered his head into his hands and sobbed, they began to pray. "God help us," they called out as Carol played the old hymn "I Need Thee Every Hour."

Suddenly the young usher came running down the aisle, embracing the others. He began to cry as he looked at Jim and said, "I'm sorry. I'm sorry. I took the money. I won't do it again."

It was a confession before the Lord. But in that tearful moment as the small congregation simply hugged each other and prayed together in earnest, Jim felt a spiritual breakthrough.

The next one came a few weeks later. Again he was in tears as he beseeched the Lord for a visitation of the Holy Spirit.

"Lord, I have no idea how to be a successful pastor," he prayed softly, alone with God. "I haven't been trained. All I know is that Carol and I are working in the middle of New York City, with people dying on every side, overdosing from heroin, consumed by materialism, and all the rest. If the gospel is so powerful . . ."

He had to stop. Tears choked him.

Then, forcefully from deep within his spirit, he sensed God speaking to him.

"If you and your wife will lead My people to pray and to call My name, you will never lack for something fresh to preach. I will supply all the money that's needed, both for the church and for your family, and you will never have a building large enough to contain the crowds I will send in response." [3]

Jim knew he had heard from God. He was telling him that transforming power would result from his tiny congregation banding together and calling out to Him in prayer.

For the first time, Jim looked forward to preaching that coming Sunday.

In the weeks that followed, there were many answers to prayers. Family members would bring new people. Strangers began showing up. God kept increasing the congregation. He brought talented people to sing and play instruments. He grew the church just like He said He would.

The famous Brooklyn Tabernacle today has sixteen thousand members and is one of the biggest churches in the Greater New York area. It is noted for its Grammy Award–winning Brooklyn Tabernacle Choir, under the direction of Carol Cymbala.

Jim Cymbala has been the pastor of the church for more than forty years.

PETER VINCENT: THE VACATION THAT WAS ANYTHING BUT

It was the first major vacation they had taken in several years. Peter and Missy Vincent, accompanied by little Peter, age eleven, and Missy's mom, Judy Norton, were excited. The travel agent had gotten them a good deal at a resort in the Dominican Republic. And when friends from their church, Mark Crossland and his wife, Bernie, heard about it, they changed their plans to travel to another Caribbean island in order to meet up with the Vincents.

Little did they all know that a nightmare was awaiting them.

A few days before leaving their home on Martha's Vineyard, Peter had a scheduled medical checkup; he had experienced off and on again high blood pressure and wanted to get it checked. His attention to such matters had been heightened seven years earlier when a heart blockage had been discovered, requiring five stents.

His medical exam appeared to be normal.

Their first three days in the Dominican Republic were delightful. However, on the fourth evening, they went out for dinner and Peter became exceptionally tired, and began to have difficulty walking. Then, back at their room, he collapsed on the bathroom floor.

The Crosslands, whose room was but a short walk away, were quickly summoned and assisted getting Peter to a bed as Missy called for a doctor. Then the rude awakenings began. The doctor would not come to treat Peter unless his fee was paid up front. Subsequently, transportation to the hospital cost eight hundred dollars and when they got to the hospital, another five thousand dollars was required up front, which Missy had to spread over, and nearly deplete, two credit cards.

It was almost midnight when they were able to get Peter to the hospital and doctors in the intensive care unit were able to assess his condition. His blood pressure had plummeted to extremely low levels and it appeared that he had fluid in the lungs. The next report from doctors was an excruciating twelve hours later. But communication was extremely difficult. Everyone spoke Spanish only.

A saving grace, and a small godwink, occurred when Mark Crossland told Missy about an app called Google Translate that would interpret a voice and convert it to English in real time. By holding her cell phone up to the doctor and reading the screen, Missy was able to hear what the medical team was reporting. She learned, "Your husband's condition is very, very bad."

In assessing bits and pieces of information, she concluded the doctors were simply incapable of treating Peter and that many medicines used in the Dominican Republic were considered antiquated by standards in the States. She was advised of another hospital that was better equipped, but a two-and-a-half-hour ambulance ride away in Santo Domingo, over difficult and potted roads. She wondered how much better it was.

Worried sick, Missy's prayers for Peter elevated in frequency and urgency. They were *spoken* in earnest, as she was joined by her mother, Judy, and the Crosslands, all prayer warriors.

Finally, Missy was able to get in to see her husband, who was barely conscious, and she and Peter prayed together.

Missy made two important calls: she was able to reach a consul at the American embassy who promised to come to the hospital, help interpret, and provide options. And she reached out to Don Bradley, pastor of her church, Beacon of Hope, on Martha's Vineyard. Don triggered the prayer line and within minutes, word spread as friends went into urgent prayer for Peter.

The consul arrived and brought with him an embassy-published list of local contacts but had no suggestions on how Peter could be transported out of the Dominican Republic to an American hospital in Miami.

At the bottom of the list Missy noticed a handwritten notation, "Med Eval," and a phone number. It had a different area code.

"What's that?" she asked.

The consul didn't know.

Something inside caused her to dial the number. A man answered, in English. He said he was in Miami.

"Oh," she said, processing. "What does 'Med Eval' mean?"

"I think you mean 'medical evacuation,'" he replied.

Missy's eyes widened. "Yes! How can I evacuate my husband from the Dominican Republic to a hospital in Miami?"

Paperwork and conferences with the hospital staff were all required, he said, plus the big item. "We'll need a down payment of twenty-one thousand dollars."

Missy knew she didn't have that kind of credit left on her charge card. What to do?

In a continued thread of divine alignment, Mark Crossland happened to be standing next to her as she spoke to the medical evacuation man in Miami. "Just do it," Mark kept saying, assuring her that he would cover the costs on his credit card.

Some twenty-four hours after Peter's initial heart attack, he still lacked the basic medical treatments that were considered necessary in the States; his blood pressure remained dangerously low, and his body was beginning to shut down. The first signs were renal failure—dysfunctional kidneys.

She texted Pastor Don with the updates for the Beacon of Hope prayer team. Each time a new email or text arrived, the entire congregation went on high alert and prayed.

Missy continued to speak with God and counted the minutes as she awaited notification that the jet had arrived at the airport, twenty minutes away, to take her and Peter on the two-hour flight to Kendall Regional Medical Center in Miami.

"Father God, you are in control," she kept repeating, "please keep my husband alive."

Our little church, Beacon of Hope, on Martha's Vineyard, had grown to seventy-five attendees in less than a year. It is a spirit-filled praying congregation. In their short time together, members had received one godwink blessing after another.

The most challenging task for any church is recruiting a high-quality pastor. But the first major godwink was an encounter between ourselves and Don Bradley and his wife, Gayle; he had just retired to the island after spending twenty-three years building a church of 350 in South Hadley, Massachusetts. In the faith-barren northeastern corner of the United States, a church of 400 is jokingly tagged as "mega."

"Have you ever thought of throwing your hat in the ring to pastor a church here?" asked Louise casually, even though she had just met the man.

"Yes," said Don almost immediately. We each noticed Gayle's eyebrows lift, as if to say, *Really?*

We had no way of knowing that just weeks before, Don and Gayle had had a momentous event in their lives. Their grandson Luke had been declared cancer-free after battling leukemia for more than three years. Month after month Don had prayed passionately, asking God to heal his sweet grandson, promising, "God, if you heal Luke, I will do anything you ask."

Who knew that God would select Louise to do the "asking"? For when the Bradleys encountered us, and Louise popped the question "Would you pastor a church on the island?" Don immediately interpreted the words she *spoke* as God-directed.

Three days later, we learned that a new church on our faith-starved island was in need of a pastor. We conveyed the conversation about Don, the various parties got together, and the divine dots were connected.

Now Pastor Don was rallying his new church family for Peter and Missy. The Beacon of Hope prayer line continued to buzz with fervor, passing the word to pray for Peter's survival and peace for Missy.

As the medical evacuation jet from the Dominican Republic arrived in Miami, Missy felt a false sense of security, thinking her husband now had a chance to get the kind of treatment he needed, and that they would soon be on their way home.

However, another crushing reality was waiting. Doctors rushed Peter into ICU for diagnosis and soon Missy was being told that he was in critical condition with only a 10 percent chance of survival.

"Your husband is very sick," said the doctor. "If you have family, they should come see him now."

Missy quickly texted that information to the Beacon of Hope prayer team. Again the clarions were sounded. The beseeching for God to save Peter were *spoken* from the lips of our congregation.

Within twenty-four hours, there were more dreaded words assaulting Missy: "Your husband coded." That's a medical term for "Your husband died, was brought back to life, and he's barely hanging on."

Peter's daughters Eve and Stephanie arrived from the Vineyard, and soon they were all praying for a miraculous turnaround.

For the next two weeks Missy kept texting the prayer line leaders at Beacon of Hope whenever there was specific prayer needed, and each time the small army opened their texts or email, they cried out to God.

On the fourteenth day after he arrived at Kendall Hospital, Peter opened his eyes. Slowly, God had started rewarding the requests of prayers that were spoken by Peter's family, the small church of believers, and many others in the island community. Soon the "evidence of things not seen" was the recompense for their faith. Peter was making a recovery, and the Kendall staff members began to label him their "miracle patient."

"This is almost unheard of, after what your husband has been through," said one nurse to Missy.

"You shouldn't be here," said another male nurse to Peter, explaining that he had been at Peter's side when he first arrived. "I can't believe you're here," he repeated.

Peter smiled. He looked at the nurse's name tag. It was "Jesus"!

He knew this was a godwink from above; the real Jesus had made it possible for him to come back among the living.

After another week he was able to fly home, where he spent two more weeks at the Martha's Vineyard hospital.

Peter was able to start putting together the pieces of his journey. He was starting to verbalize experiences he didn't quite know how to talk about.

"I went to a place with gigantic white buildings," he recalls, believing it was when he died. "They seemed Roman or Greek—in white marble. But the bright whiteness was coming through the buildings, not from within. I felt a great presence with me as I looked at hundreds of statues . . . well, I *thought* they were statues . . . but they were of people, all looking their best, who looked like they were in the midst of movement when I arrived, but, like a stop-action movie, my time was out of sync with theirs. Time and space seemed different. A second could be a hundred years."

Did you want to leave there? we asked.

"I wanted to come back and see my family, but my perspective has changed."

"How's that?"

"I have no fear of death now."

At Beacon of Hope Church, the congregation stood in applause as Peter walked in with a cane a few weeks later.

Another victory had been scored for this praying church; they had once again "stormed the gates of heaven" with prayer, and the list of healings, miracles, and unbelievable godwinks was continuing to grow.

JOHN SMITH: A TAPESTRY OF MIRACLES

What a day! It was an unusually balmy January 19—55 degrees—tying the record for the warmest in years.

Fourteen-year-old John Smith and three friends were off from school that Monday afternoon, Martin Luther King Jr. Day, walking along the shores of Lake Saint Louis, Missouri.

This upscale city of fifteen thousand was birthed as a planned community in the mid-1960s when the founders flooded six hundred acres to create a magnificent recreational lake.

Cold weeks in December and early January had frozen the lake, and the boys, John and two others, both named Josh, felt an enticing temptation: to test the ice. In shirtsleeves, the trio ventured onto the ice, leaving Jamie Rieger, a sister of one of the boys, on shore. They went out farther and farther. At one hundred fifty feet from shore everything seemed fine.

Then . . . *CRACK!* The ice split! All three plunged into the cold water!

Josh Sanders managed to crawl out, grasping the hand of Josh Rieger, helping him out. But John Smith had disappeared into the dark, freezing water under the ice.

Panic-stricken, the boys called to Jaime, who called 911.

The Lake Saint Louis Fire Department rescue vehicle was speeding the short distance to the scene as Captain Justin Darnell pondered the thought: the 911 call said a boy had gone under the ice. Yet how ironic that *something* had nudged him late in the prior week to schedule an ice-rescue training session for the first time in more than a year. They had just completed it on Saturday, forty-eight hours before.

He felt encouraged that his team would be ready to do the best possible job without losing precious seconds: getting out the gear, slipping into wet suits, quickly loading a victim on the ice sled . . . they'd rehearsed everything, including hand signals. The drills were fresh in mind. *What are the chances of that?* he thought.

Fireman Tommie Shine rapidly got into his wet suit and moved cautiously across the ice, carrying a twelve-foot fiberglass pole with a hooked end.

He knew this lake well. Lake Saint Louis was fifty feet deep and muddy at the bottom in most places. In others, it was only ten feet with a rock bottom.

As he approached the break in the ice, *something* nudged him to lower his pole where he did.

Almost immediately he felt a soft object. Miraculously, he was able to hook onto it. Had he caught onto the boy's clothing?

He had! They pulled the boy onto the ice. Moments later John Smith was strapped to the ice sled and moving toward the waiting ambulance and the EMS crew. Only twenty minutes had elapsed, they estimated, since John Smith had fallen under the ice.

He was rushed to the nearest hospital, Saint Joseph Hospital West, where head emergency room doctor, Kent Sutterer, was alerted and standing by with his team. A dozen or so emergency room physicians, respiratory technicians, nurses, and paramedics worked feverishly for another twenty minutes, without success.

Later Dr. Sutterer wrote in a personal letter to record the event that "the boy had remained pulseless" for forty minutes plus transportation time, the better part of an hour.

In addition to constant CPR, Dr. Sutterer tried to raise John Smith's body temperature—getting it up to 95 degrees. The doctor had learned that "you're not dead until you're warm and dead." But the outcome was becoming clear; they had "exhausted all interventions in their scientific toolkit . . . without even a hint of success."

Dr. Sutterer began to think that it was time for him to declare death. He asked someone to bring in the boy's mother.

Joyce Smith came to her son's bedside, where she noted his gray and motionless body, but was not about to accept a verdict of death.

Her Bible class was using Beth Moore's study guide, which teaches that "God is who He says He is, and God can do what He says He can do."

She also studied Proverbs 18:21: "Death and Life are in the power of the tongue."

With firm words supporting those principles, Joyce Smith looked at her son and *spoke* loudly: "God, send your Holy Spirit to heal my son."

Instantly a technician said, "We've got a pulse!"

Nurses began to cry.

The room was reenergized.

Joyce had spoken it, believed it, and expected that outcome!

Dr. Sutterer wrote, "That boy's heart was jump-started by the Holy Spirit listening to the request of a praying mother."

"I know that God has given us a gift . . . I was privileged to witness a miracle."

With a pulse, they were able to airlift John Smith to the St. Louis children's hospital, Cardinal Glennon. He maintained a heartbeat but was still in a coma.

At John Smith's church, First Assembly of Saint Peters, MO, a prayer vigil was quickly organized. Word went out immediately on social media that John Smith was in the hospital, but, miraculously, his heartbeat had returned.

John Smith's pastor at First Assembly Church, Jason Noble, arrived at the hospital and joined five other pastors around the boy's bed.

The young pastor and his wife, Paula, had moved to Saint Peters with their four children only seven months earlier from Washington State.

Jason was told that doctors feared that John's brain was damaged beyond repair. So, standing on the left side of the bed and *speaking* into the boy's right ear, Jason led prayers beseeching the Holy Spirit to specifically reconstruct John's brain and lungs. They prayed and prayed.

Something caused Jason to turn to look at the men at the end of the bed. But . . . beyond them . . . he saw two bright white angels standing against the back of the room! The others didn't see the angels, but Jason says he recognized them.

"When I was in Washington State I had been praying over a woman who was given only fifteen minutes to live. I looked up and saw two angels—the same angels—standing in her room. The woman instantly began to get well. She lives today."

As Jason resumed his prayer over John Smith he had a renewed sense that God was answering his prayer right then and there . . . restitching the boy's brain and lungs.

"It feels like electricity is in the air," said the pastor on the right side of the bed.

Jason Noble then saw what he described as a ring of thousands of colored lights around John's head . . . like laser lights.

Suddenly the boy squeezed Jason's hand, opened his eyes, lifted his shoulders up off the bed, and then lay back down and closed his eyes.

In that moment Pastor Jason's *expectation* that John Smith would live came to pass. He did! On the third day, John awoke and responded to verbal and written commands.

The head doctor at Cardinal Glennon, Jeremy Garrett, a recent Pediatrician of the Year, again surprised many as he boldly spoke as a physician. He said: "This is a miraculous story from our Heavenly Father to a fourteen-year-old boy named John Smith."

John's father, Brian Smith, summed up the extraordinary series of events with this statement: "Sixteen days after he was under a frozen lake, my son walked out of the hospital under his own steam; with no signs of brain damage; no damage to his lungs. In fact, he's back to normal playing basketball."

This miracle, said Brian, was in great part due to the praying church. He said on the evening of the tragedy the church prayer warriors went into action. More than three hundred people gathered at the church agreed to pray specifically for John, and the clarion for prayer was rapidly spread over social media to far corners of the globe.

"We heard from people in Germany who were praying for John," says his father, "while others in Illinois were constantly asking our relatives there how John was doing."

Nine weeks after his drowning, John Smith looked out shyly to the congregation of First Assembly Church. Pastor Jason had invited the family and all the first responders to share their testimony.

Every member of the congregation—and hundreds more in the community and around the globe—felt a personal connection with the boy for whom they had prayed fervently. His presence on that platform was evidence that their prayers were answered.

"Thank you for your prayers. I thank the Lord for my life," said John in a sweet voice.

Describe what great things God has done for you.
—LUKE 8:39

THE ROLE OF ANGELS AND YOUR PRAYERS

Praying at John Smith's bedside, Jason Noble "looked up and saw two angels," which he's convinced are the same two angels he'd seen before when he prayed over a woman in Washington State who was healed immediately thereafter.

In both cases, the angelic appearances were seen only by Jason. In both cases, they appeared while Jason was fervently praying. And in both cases, the person was completely healed.

Billy Graham once described angels as "God's secret agents."

We are told in the ancient scriptures that God "will command his angels . . . to guard you in all your ways . . . they will lift you up in their hands." [4]

How significant are angels in the Bible? They are mentioned 273 times.

Seventy-seven percent of the people polled by the E. W. Scripps School of Journalism at Ohio University believe that angels are some kind of heavenly beings that visit the earth. Another 20 percent of the 1,127 respondents believe that angels walk among us.

That data parallels an oft-quoted verse in Hebrews suggesting you most likely have encountered an angel face-to-face without realizing it, as they carry out their work like God's undercover Secret Service: "Show hospitality to strangers, for by so doing, some people have shown hospitality to angels without knowing it."[5]

Another study by Baylor University's Institute for Studies of Religion, reported in *Time* magazine, found that 55 percent of 1,700 respondents affirmed that "I was protected from harm by a guardian angel."[6]

Although angels are wonderful blessings from God, we are reminded that we must never pray to them. Praying to anyone other than God is idolatry.

John testified about his angelic encounter in Revelation. But when he "fell down to worship at the feet of the angel," the angel responded, "You must not do that! I am a fellow servant with you . . . worship God."[7]

TOM RENFRO: THE AWESOME POWER OF A PRAYING CHURCH

Dr. Tom Renfro lives in the small community of Norton, Virginia, population 4,500. He's a well-respected physician, loved by many.

When his town heard the terrible news that Tom had been diagnosed with mantle cell lymphoma, stage 4—the final stages of the cancer—they were devastated.

Confirmed by the University of Virginia, Dr. Renfro's alma mater, he was told there was no cure—that this type of lymphoma often marches right through chemotherapy, and that bone marrow and stem cell transplants generally fail to cure this kind of disease. "Go home and enjoy what time you have left," they advised.

Tom's oncologist, Dr. Steven Woodley, also leveled with him: "Once you reach this extensive stage of the disease, odds are approaching zero that you'll ever be disease-free."

Tom made a decision that may have seemed odd at the time; to videotape his last few months of life. Over the next few weeks, as the cancer progressed, it was painful to see how it ravaged his body.

Above the surface, the videotape revealed baseball-size tumors quickly popping up all over; in his neck, under his arms and abdomen. Beneath the surface, blood clots were targeting his lungs and heart. He was beginning to have multi-organ failure, malnutrition, and ulcers.

How could this hopeless story ever turn to hope?

Prayer.

The stubborn, nonstop prayers of a believing church!

Tom's congregation refused to give up on him. They loved him and committed to pray for him for twelve hours a day for forty days. Often people prayed throughout the night. When they reached the end of forty days—just the way Moses returned to the Mountain of God a second time—they started praying another forty days, all over again.

It seemed as though the more the church prayed, the worse he got. Still, they dug in their heels and prayed more.

When Tom's kidneys began to fail, doctors knew the end was near. Now their short-range goal was simply to keep him alive until Christmas. Their last-ditch plan was to squeeze out a few more days of life by administering chemotherapy.

Yet before the chemo even began, something miraculous happened.

Tom's wife, Sid, said she witnessed the most powerful manifestation of the Holy Spirit she's ever seen: "All of a sudden, the tumors melted away. They were gone! There was no more cancer!"

Tom's army of prayer warriors at church felt the utter joy of witnessing the power of their relentless beseeching to the Lord.

His friend and physician, Dr. Jack Cox, said, "I felt that Tom was miraculously cured and, through his faith, God worked to preserve his life."

A mere two weeks later Tom stood in front of his church, tearfully expressing his joy. "I want you to understand that this is a true miracle. This is what you have been praying for! I don't have the words to express what is in my heart, nor what God has done for me, but you are looking at a true miracle of God!"

If Tom hadn't videotaped his journey, most people simply wouldn't have believed it. But the town of Norton and the surrounding county saw for themselves what can happen when a praying church is faithful to the power of God; their prayers were answered when an Almighty God intervened and saved a friend who was given no hope.

A few months later Tom and Sid headed to Israel, where he was baptized in the Jordan River. With arms raised in victory, he shouted, through tears of joy, "Glory to God! Glory to God!"

Once again healthy, Dr. Tom is doing today what he does best: helping others to get well.

WHY DOES GOD CHOOSE TO HEAL SOME PEOPLE BUT NOT OTHERS?

No one will be able to answer that question with certainty until we sit at the feet of the Lord and ask Him.

Persistence of prayer and the expectation of a successful outcome surely play critical roles in individual cases, but part of the mystery of God is why he allows some to be healed and not others.

Even the apostle Paul, who had amazing faith, did not get healed after he asked God three times. We can only trust that God is aware of our suffering and has a higher purpose for it.

We can conclude that one of God's reasons for the healing of Dr. Tom Renfro was so Tom would tell as many people as possible about his experiences.

> *Nothing tends more to cement the hearts of Christians*
> *than praying together. Never do they love one another*
> *so well as when they witness the outpouring of each*
> *other's hearts in prayer.*[8]
> —CHARLES FINNEY

CHAPTER 5

WHEN OUR NATION PRAYED

Follow all his commands . . . the Lord your God
will set you high above all the nations on earth.
—DEUTERONOMY 21:1, NIV

CAN AN ENTIRE NATION BENEFIT FROM THE POWER OF PRAYER?

It has already happened.

While trying to draft the US Constitution, the Founding Fathers were locked in an impossible logjam. They had been debating exhaustively for five weeks. The eleventh anniversary of America's independence was only days away, and the leaders could find no way to break the perilous deadlock.

The same leaders who only a few years earlier had the temerity to declare independence from the most powerful nation on earth and succeeded, who dared to engage Great Britain's professional army in a war and won, were now like disagreeable climbers mired at the foot of an unscalable mountain.

An eighty-one-year-old man with flowing gray hair and wire spectacles—quiet for much of the debate—rose slowly to his feet.

His mythological stature as a statesman, as an ambassador, inventor, and writer, commanded the attention of all. Perhaps only he, Benjamin Franklin, could have had the audacity, during that moment of boiling tempers, to suggest that what they must now do . . . was to pray.[1]

He reminded his colleagues that during the war they had beseeched God on a daily basis. "Our prayers were heard, sirs, and they were graciously answered," he *spoke* confidently, turning his body to engage each and every member of his audience.

"Have we now forgotten that powerful friend? Or do we imagine that we no longer need His assistance?"

Certain that every eye and ear was attentive, the elder statesman delivered the *spoken words* that penetrated the heavy air of stalemate with grace and logic, enduring as one of the most quotable moments of the Constitutional Convention.

"I have lived, sirs, a long time; and the longer I live, the more convincing proofs I see of this truth—that God governs in the affairs of men. And if a sparrow cannot fall to the ground without His notice, is it probable that an empire can rise without His aid?"

Benjamin Franklin moved to begin every session with prayer "imploring the assistance of Heaven."

His motion did not carry. It was not even voted upon. Perhaps too many of the lawmakers were rigidly irascible or stubbornly proud to succumb to such a simple plan of grace. They did not honor him.

But God did.

Many devout statesmen present that day reported that shortly after Franklin's speech, the deadlock mysteriously broke, and America had a Constitution.

Can we conclude that members of eight differing denominations prayed together in private, rather than praying together publicly?[2] And that God honored each of them, as well as Franklin?

David Barton, one of America's most meticulous historians, has a personal collection of more than one hundred thousand documents—books, letters, and journals, many in the original handwriting of America's founders. He provides persuasive evidence that Franklin's call for his colleagues to pray together "is just one example of how answered prayer changed the course of the nation."[3]

Barton quotes Benjamin Rush, an observer of the Constitutional Convention and one of the original signers of the Declaration of Independence: "I am as perfectly satisfied that the Union of the States in its form and adoption, is as much the work of a Divine Providence, as any of the miracles recorded in the Old and New Testament were the effects of a Divine power."[4]

Delegate Alexander Hamilton said, "I sincerely esteem it a system which, without the finger of God, never could have been suggested and agreed upon by such a diversity of interests."[5]

Barton credits James Madison, another delegate, for this comment: "It is impossible for the man of pious reflection not to perceive it a finger of that Almighty Hand, which has been so frequently and signally extended to our relief, in the critical stages of the Revolution."[6]

George Washington, who presided over the Constitutional Convention, added, "As to my sentiments with respect to the merits of the new Constitution, I will disclose them without reserve . . . it appears to me then, little short of a miracle, that the delegates from so many different states . . . should unite in forming a system of national government."

Yet David Barton laments that as the godly passions of our

Founding Fathers erode with time and cultural changes, our nation becomes more and more vulnerable: "When a country drifts away from God, God drifts away from that country."

In the following century, Abraham Lincoln decried that God was systematically diminished in America. The Civil War president, quoted by Barton, said, "We have forgotten God. We have forgotten the gracious hand which preserved us in peace and multiplied and enriched and strengthened us . . . we have vainly imagined in the deceitfulness of our hearts that all these blessings were produced by some superior wisdom and virtue of our own. Intoxicated with unbroken success, we have become too self-sufficient to feel the necessity of redeeming and preserving—too proud to pray to the God that made us."[7]

> *"Work as if you were to live a hundred years, pray as if you were to die tomorrow."*
> *—Benjamin Franklin*

ARE YOU BULLETPROOF?

In most of our lives, our crazy adolescence was the time when we were likely to test the boundaries of our mortality. How daring we could be in a drag race or jumping from a dangerous precipice into a swimming hole was more to impress our peers than an action of rational thinking. As teenagers, many kids think they are bulletproof—and that they'll live forever.

Sadly, so many who have tested this theory by driving speeding cars and taking drugs have been proven wrong.

The next story begs the question, What made George Washington bulletproof and not everyone else?

How could Washington, a tall man, astride a horse on a field of battle—a perfect target for the enemy—emerge unscathed so many times?

How did he finish one battle with four bullet holes in his coat but no wounds . . . even though one marksman testified that he'd aimed and mysteriously missed seventeen times and another eleven times?

When you read this account told to us by historian David Barton, perhaps you too will conclude that George Washington's daily regimen of prayer was the reason for his amazing coat of armor.

THE LEGEND OF THE BULLETPROOF GEORGE WASHINGTON

Twenty years before the Revolutionary War, the British and French, having fought it out in three previous wars, were again squabbling, this time over land claims in western Pennsylvania. The French banded together with large Native American tribes with the aim of claiming all American territory west of the Allegheny Mountains.[8] This stirred the ire of the British crown.

The governor of Virginia, on behalf of the empire, wrote a stern warning to the French commander, stationed near what is now Pittsburgh, demanding no further encroachment.

To deliver the message, he called upon twenty-one-year-old George Washington, who had demonstrated exceptional leadership in Virginia military matters. Designated as an ambassador,[9] Washington rode five hundred miles through the wilderness only to be rebuffed by the French commander, but his handling of the matter had greatly impressed his countrymen.

A few months later, a regiment of thirteen hundred British troops landed in Virginia and was preparing to retake the territory by force. Washington was named a lieutenant colonel and put in charge of one hundred Virginia recruits who were to accompany the British. He was to offer counsel and to serve General Edward Braddock.[10]

Still weary from a high fever and an illness that kept him in bed for more than a week, Washington quickly determined that Braddock, a longtime veteran of European-style wars in which both sides openly faced each other and shot it out, had very little regard for the American "Buckskins." Nor did he heed Washington's advice to send a scouting party of friendly Native Americans to determine where the French were located.

Seven miles from the French fort where the Allegheny and Monongahela Rivers meet, the thirteen hundred king's troops marched in precise order through a wooded ravine, their bright red uniforms offering a picture of grandeur against the dark foliage, as the gay sounds of fife and drums kept them moving with military pomp.[11] The one hundred Americans were to the rear.

It was in that picturesque setting that about half that many troops, two hundred French soldiers and six hundred Native Americans, lay in wait among the trees. In a torrent of gunfire, pouring down from both sides of the ravine, the British troops were cut down like toy soldiers.

Eighty-six officers on horseback bravely rode up and down, ordering their troops to stand and fight; according to British tradition, running for cover was dishonorable and forbidden. They stood, huddled together, shooting at unseen targets, and falling in massive numbers.[12]

Washington was the general's liaison, repeatedly riding his

horse through a storm of bullets to deliver Braddock's orders to other officers.

Washington had two horses shot from under him. He would immediately mount the horse of a fallen British officer and resume his duties.

Two hours later, 714 British troops had been shot down and seventy of the one hundred colonists. The French and Native Americans had but thirty casualties. It was a massive rout, with each of the eighty-six British officers and Braddock being shot. In fact, George Washington was the only officer who was not wounded and was still mounted on a horse.[13]

As the bedraggled survivors limped back toward Virginia, Washington had to stop midway to tend to his illness for several days. While recuperating, he wrote letters to comfort his mother and his brother.[14]

Although death was leveling my companions on every side of me . . . I escaped without a wound; however, I had four bullets through my coat and two horses shot from under me. By the all-powerful dispensations of Providence I have been protected beyond all human probability or expectation.

George Washington didn't question for a moment that it was God—not his own skills—that had saved him. This became more apparent when a Native American warrior who was a leader in the attack, later said, "Washington was never born to be killed by a bullet. I had seventeen fair fires at him with my rifle and I could not bring him to the ground."[15]

Another legendary Native American named Red Hawk, who had a reputation for never missing his mark, said that after failing to kill Washington with eleven shots, he ceased trying, being convinced that Washington was protected by the Great Spirit.[16]

Fifteen years after what had become known as the Battle at Monongahela, George Washington was traveling through the Western Territories. He and his party were approached by a company of Native Americans led by an older, highly respected chief. The chief had learned that Washington was near and felt compelled to personally speak with "the young warrior of the great battle."

He recalled the day that his tribes had joined the French at that wooded ravine.[17] "I called to my young men and said, 'Mark yon tall and daring warrior . . . he is not of the red-coat tribe . . . let your aim be certain, and he dies. Our rifles were leveled . . . we knew not how to miss . . . but a power mightier than we, shielded you."

The elder chief then provided Washington with a prophecy. Still six years before the Declaration of Independence, he pointed at Washington and said, "The Great Spirit protects that man and guides his destinies. He will become the chief of nations and people yet unborn will hail him as the founder of a mighty empire . . . I am come to pay homage to the man who is a particular favorite of Heaven and who can never die in battle."

The common threads woven through this remarkable story—and George Washington's entire life—are those of a man who was raised to put his trust in God and who treated God as a daily companion through earnest prayer. As a result, the man who fulfilled the Native American chief's prophecy and became our country's first president never wavered in his faith, and God never wavered in His benevolence toward him.

The fate of unborn millions will now depend, under God, on
the courage and conduct of this army.
—GEORGE WASHINGTON, AUGUST 27, 1776

For 150 years this inspiring story was available to every student of American history. Then, for the past five decades, prompted by the Supreme Court's decision to remove prayer from public schools, this vital piece of history has been erased from the sight of children—presumably for their benefit—"protecting" them under the claim that there must be a total division between church and state.

WHAT A HISTORY TEACHER DISCOVERED

David Barton was a high school history teacher when he noticed that, according to government documents, there were monumental shifts in our nation's barometers of morality, all occurring at the same time.

A coincidence?

For instance, birth rates among unwed girls age fifteen to nineteen, which had been steady at about 15.5 percent of births per 1,000 girls for the decade prior to 1963, suddenly doubled over the next two decades and rose to 45 percent by 1993.[18]

Sexually transmitted diseases among ten-to-fourteen-year-olds had declined in the eight years prior to 1963 to a low of 14 percent per 100,000. However, in the next ten years it rose to 42 percent, spiking to 70 percent in 1988.[19]

"What happened in America at the same time," asked David Barton, "that could have dramatically caused the morality standards to shift in our country?"

Can we ignore that the Supreme Court decided to deny prayer and the discussion of God in our public schools in 1963?

> *To get nations back on their feet,*
> *we must first get down on our knees.*
> —REV. BILLY GRAHAM

MILITARY LEADERS WHO PRAY

We've seen the vital role of prayer in preserving the life of George Washington, who was called "bulletproof" because he was never wounded notwithstanding the numerous occasions that enemy sharpshooters were assigned the very task of taking him out. Yet there are many other stories of leaders who rose to great heights with God always at their side.

Following is a legendary story of how prayer played a vital role in the formation of the thirty-fourth president of the United States, Dwight D. Eisenhower.

HOW PRAYER SAVED A FUTURE PRESIDENT

Doc Conklin wore a heavy frown as he examined the fourteen-year-old boy's reddened and swollen leg. For several hours, the youngster had slipped into and out of delirium with high fever. Pointing to a black streak up the thigh, the doctor's eyes shifted to the boy's mother, Ida Eisenhower.

"If the blood poisoning hits his stomach, he will die.[20] It's not likely we can save it."[21]

"What's that mean?" rasped the boy, startling the doctor, who had presumed he was in a semi-coma and would not hear him.

"It means, Dwight," said Doc Conklin, choosing his words carefully, "that . . . we may have to cut off your leg."

A look of instant shock came over Ida's countenance.

"Not me!" said Dwight firmly. "I'd rather die!"

Dwight's mind had fixed immediately on his obsession with school sports. The doctor's option to remove a leg to save his life was simply not an acceptable option.

Dr. Tracy Conklin, the country physician who traveled farm to farm calling on patients around Abilene, Kansas, motioned for Ida to follow him out of the room to speak with her privately, away from further interference from his patient.

"Ed! Ed! Come up here, will you?" Dwight hollered to his older brother Edgar.

Before his brother had fully bounded into the room, Dwight cried out in high-pitched pain. "If I go out of my head, Ed, don't let 'em cut off my leg. Promise me, Ed, promise!" [22]

Edgar promised and promptly stationed himself outside the door to the room, looking directly at Doc Conklin. "Nobody's going to saw off that leg," he repeated resolutely.

Doc Conklin's frustration and anger began to rise as he appealed to the mother and to the father, David, who had now joined them. The physician urged them to overrule the boys, contending that anything less would be "murder." [23] They declined to do so.

For several days, Edgar slept across the threshold of his brother's room in order that no one could get in without his knowledge. [24]

In subsequent days Doc Conklin returned to the Eisenhower

farm several times, once with another doctor from Topeka who joined in the appeal to the parents to let them amputate the leg, but David and Ida continued to side with the boys.

Dwight's fever mounted; he remained delirious, babbling in pain. Edgar, because he'd given his brother his promise, stood his ground staunchly. Ida and David were emboldened by their steadfast sons.[25]

The one thing they *could* do was to pray.

Dwight's grandfather was a frontier preacher who believed in healings through faith.[26] Prayer was a common occurrence.

Every member of the family prayed for Dwight's survival, taking turns, around the clock.

After three days, the fever miraculously abated, the ominous black line disappeared, and the family knew that God had intervened to save Dwight's life.

Edgar was later quoted as saying there was "a great deal of praying by everyone," adding that "Doc Conklin admitted that he had once more met the medical man's superior—God Almighty."[27]

Still, Dwight's recovery kept him out of school for the remainder of the year and he had to repeat the ninth grade.

Feeling a deep indebtedness to Edgar, says historian David Barton, Dwight offered to delay his own application to college by two years in order to work and help shoulder the costs for his older brother's college tuition.[28]

When it came time for Dwight to apply, he wrote to his US senator from Kansas and asked to be considered for either Annapolis or West Point. The Naval Academy did not permit applicants who were turning twenty, so when Dwight ranked second in a test taken by ten candidates, he was given the one spot available to West Point.[29]

When we look back upon Dwight Eisenhower's life, we have to marvel at the divinely aligned godwinks that unfolded. Had Dwight not overheard the doctor, thereby calling for his brother's aid to resolutely refuse the amputation, he could never have entered the military later on as a one-legged person. Yet that was the pathway he was destined to travel in order to become a five-star general, the supreme commander of the Allied Forces in World War II, and president of the United States.[30]

Equally important, had the family not rallied around Dwight in fervent prayer, his survival is not likely.

One can easily conclude that parents David and Ida, who had a practice of praying daily with their six children, who were desperately worried about their boy, yet who had refused two doctors permission to amputate their son's leg in order to "save his life," would indeed have marshaled the whole family into prayer teams to be on their knees, around the clock!

God shapes the world by prayer.
The more praying . . . the better the world will be,
the mightier the forces against evil.
—E. M. BOUNDS

CHAPTER 6

THE ENEMY IS REAL

IS THERE AN ENEMY OUT THERE?

Here is a basic principle of warfare.

In order to prevent yourself being overcome by an enemy, you must accept that he is there, determine who he is, understand his mission, and become knowledgeable about his tactics.

Knowing your enemy is critical to your mission, says Sun Tzu, whose classic military strategies were written in 500 BC, and admired by military leaders everywhere.

> *If you know the enemy and know yourself, you need not fear the result of a hundred battles. If you know yourself but not the enemy, for every victory gained you will also suffer a defeat. If you know neither the enemy nor yourself, you will succumb in every battle.*
> —SUN TZU, *THE ART OF WAR*[1]

Yet, would it be fair to say that most who acknowledge the grace and goodness of God in our daily lives give scant attention to our enemy?

We pray to God, as we should. We go to church and sing

about God, as we should. But how often do we even acknowledge the evil antithesis to God?

Can you say, as Sun Tzu suggests, that you "know the enemy and know yourself, [and] you need not fear the result of a hundred battles"?

If you don't know him, you can't defeat him.

KNOWING YOUR ENEMY IS NOT EASY

Who the enemy is, is not nearly as evident as *who* God is. In the Bible, the source of evil is given at least ten names: Satan, the Devil, Prince of Darkness, Antichrist, Beelzebub, Lucifer, Tempter, Accuser, Angel of Light, Deceiver, and others.

Perhaps the confusion in "what to call him" is why most people in the church simply label him "the Enemy." That, at least, helps us understand *who* we're talking about and what to call him.

Yet, what do we really *know* about him?

BASIC CHARACTERISTICS OF THE ENEMY

- He's an **indweller**. Just as the Holy Spirit dwells within you—presuming you have welcomed Him in—the Enemy dwells within those who allow him in.
- As a cunning counterfeit, expect the Enemy to appear in **disguise**. That's part of his plot to take you into his snare.
- He is always **dishonest**. Never expect truth from him.
- The enemy lives in **darkness**; in fact, one of his names is Prince of Darkness. He hates the light and runs from it, because God's light reveals the truth. He wants to pull

you into his zone of safety and comfort—the shadows and darkness.

- It is when he is free to create **disillusion**, **distraction**, or **discombobulation** that the enemy can trip you up and fill your mind with **discouragement**.

We've come to call him **"Dis of Darkness"** because "dis" is his favorite state of being.

But whatever you call him, you must never pretend he does not exist. You must know your Enemy, how he operates, and expect he is there, waiting for his opportunity to enter into your mind, body, and life.

HOW DO YOU PROTECT YOURSELF FROM THE ENEMY?

In the Bible you are told to put on the full armor of God, and keep it on, at all times.

> *For our struggle is not against flesh and blood,*
> *but against . . . the spiritual forces of wickedness.*
> *Therefore, take up the full armor of God,*
> *so you will be able to resist in the evil day,*
> *and having done everything, to stand firm.*[2]

Further, you are advised:

> *Be alert and of sober mind. Your enemy*
> *the devil prowls around like a roaring lion*
> *looking for someone to devour.*[3]

WHAT DOES GOD MEAN BY FULL ARMOR?

The scriptures are very specific. Let's take apart the armor, piece by piece:

1. "The **helmet** of salvation"[4] protects your head and mind. The Enemy will attempt to infect you with doubt and discouragement while deceitfully luring you into his snare.
2. "Take up the **shield** of faith" to protect you from "the flaming arrows of the evil one."[5] This armament protects your body from things hurled at you, venomous words, disease, or bodily blows.
3. Strap on "the **belt** of truth." The best access to God's truth is through prayer and the scriptures. When the Devil tried to tempt Jesus in the desert, he responded, "It is written."[6]
4. Put in place "the **breastplate** of righteousness";[7] in other words, always do the right thing.
5. Pick up "the **sword** of the Spirit which is the Word of God,"[8] described as "sharper than any double-edged sword."[9]

When you imagine yourself being wrapped in the full armor of God, throughout the day, every day, you are prepared to enter into the world where the Enemy lays in wait for you.

TO FIRE YOUR WEAPONS: SPEAK IT

When Christ was confronted by the Enemy, what did He do? He *spoke* it.

"Get behind me, Satan!"

His disciple Peter had just challenged the Lord's conclusions. And, surmising that the Enemy had found his way into the mind of Peter, "Jesus turned and *spoke*, not to his friend Peter, but directly to the Enemy who was inside Peter. 'Get behind me, Satan! . . . You do not have in mind the concerns of God, but merely human concerns." [10]

He further *spoke* it in this manner: "Away from me, Satan! For it is written: 'Worship the Lord your God, and serve him only.' " [11]

Jesus was using the mighty weaponry that we each have at our disposal: He *spoke* it and He employed what was "sharper than any double-edged sword"—words of the scriptures that are alive and powerful.

The Enemy, on the other hand, is the father of lies. The way to conquer him is to continue *speaking* God's word of truth.

The primary message of this book is that when you join forces with someone you love, your family member or your friend, and commit to regular prayer together and scripture reading, you are multiplying exponentially the might of your armament against the Enemy. Two are much better than one.

Five of you will chase a hundred,
and a hundred of you will chase ten thousand,
and your enemies will fall by the sword before you.
—LEVITICUS 26:8, NIV

HOW MUCH POWER DOES HE HAVE?

Most of the power the Enemy ever has . . . is what you give him.

If the Enemy is in your house, in your church, or in your

business, it's because he probably tricked you into thinking he was something he wasn't. Because of the cunning counterfeit he is, he may have slipped under the radar of your warning system.

He may have pierced your security perimeters by posing as a friend of a friend, as a charming volunteer, or as someone who was only too glad to help. The Enemy almost always travels within a host carrier, like a Trojan horse, attempting to manipulate you with his lies and infect you with his phony enchantment.

Perhaps you have been subjected to that.

Was there a time in your life when you found yourself keeping secrets from friends and family? You were too scared to reveal the truth and consequently became trapped in a web of despair?

Were you—or are you—snared by addictive behaviors? You never meant to allow yourself to get tangled so deeply, but before you knew it, things were out of your control, with no easy escape.

How did it start? Didn't someone lure you into it?

If only you knew then what you know now. You could have done what the ancient scriptures advise: "Submit yourself to God . . . then . . . resist the devil, and he will flee from you." [12]

The moment a pornographic picture pops up on the computer screen—resist!

The moment that overzealous guy says something is going to be "fantastic" for you—resist!

The moment someone tells you something is going to be so easy—a no-lose proposition—resist!

Once you resist, moving from the shadows back into the light, your hindsight will be clearer, and you'll be grateful those experiences are in your rearview mirror. These wise words will become your slogan: "The truth will set you free!" [13]

You will comprehend that, other than the ability to trick you, seduce you, con you, or to lie to you, the Enemy is really power-less. Only when you walk through a door he's opened for you—or you open a door and allow him in—is he able to weave a web of entrapment for you.

When you put his peashooter up against the nuclear might of God Almighty at your disposal, there's no contest. In your hol-sters you have Jesus on one side and the Holy Spirit on the other; and all the way, you are on God's Positioning System, the greatest GPS in existence.

When you are wrapped in the full armor of God and discharge your weaponry—*speaking* the piercing words of the ancient scrip-tures—the Enemy becomes a wimpy, toothless tiger.

BE ON THE LOOKOUT

There is a vile demonic spirit that the Enemy sets loose, partic-ularly in churches, taking root in people who knowingly or un-knowingly allow it. It's identified as the Jezebel spirit, and while it inhabits women more frequently, it also inhabits some men.

This evil spirit has been recognized since the biblical times of David. Jesus warned about it. Yet John Paul Jackson, in his book *Unmasking the Jezebel Spirit*, says few people truly understand how this demonic force operates.

THE PROFILE OF JEZEBEL

"The spirit of Jezebel is like the story of Dr. Jekyll and Mr. Hyde," says Jennifer LeClaire, who writes about this agent of the Enemy in *The Spiritual Warrior's Guide to Defeating Jezebel*.[14] "The Jezebel spirit may try to push its agenda gently at first, but if the target does not cooperate, it quickly escalates its evil plot."

LeClaire quotes nineteenth-century French poet Charles Baudelaire, who said, "Satan's greatest deception is convincing the world he does not exist."[15] If that is true, then perhaps Jezebel's greatest deception is convincing the Church that these individuals are harmless.

The Jezebel spirit aims to infiltrate a church, targeting the pastor and others in authority. If it can strike the shepherd, then the sheep will scatter. The Enemy uses someone who looks good and sounds good, so you'll assume they are good. Hindsight shows you cannot go by sight. The spirit is an excellent counterfeit. It will come as an "angel of light."

Robert Morris, pastor of Gateway Church in Dallas, says there was a season in which a Jezebel spirit was functioning in his church. He was personally attacked; often overcome by thoughts of quitting, depression, and even a desire to die. Morris says you will see the true color of a person moving in the spirit of Jezebel "after he or she gains the upper hand. And to gain the upper hand, it will latch on to people already in authority."[16]

How Do You Identify a Jezebel Spirit?

Steve Sampson, author of several books on the Jezebel spirit including *Confronting Jezebel*,[17] has compiled a comprehensive checklist to help you spot this devious culprit. Sampson, along with all the other experts quoted here, caution that we not jump to conclusions about people who have a few of the Jezebel characteristics. You need to take action only after you and others have fervently prayed about it and then conclude that there is a consistent pattern reflecting many of the following signals.

Here are twenty of Sampson's top thirty ways to spot a Jezebel:

1. Refuses to admit guilt or wrongdoing.

   A Jezebel spirit is never wrong, unless it is a temporary admission of guilt to gain "favor" with someone. To accept responsibility would violate the core of insecurity and pride from which it operates. When a Jezebel apologizes, it is never in true repentance or acknowledgment of wrongdoing, but rather, "I'm sorry your feelings were hurt."

2. Takes credit for everything.

   While a strong trait of Jezebels is never to take responsibility for their wrong actions or behavior, they are also quick to take credit for a benefit to which they contributed no effort.

3. Uses other people to accomplish its agenda.

   The Jezebel spirit lets others do its dirty work. The Jezebel gets another person's emotions stirred up, then lets that person go into a rage. The Jezebel sits back looking innocent, asking, "Who, me? What did I do?" This behavior makes it difficult for even the most ardent truth-seekers to pin one down. The Jezebel spirit is clever in its agenda.

4. Withholds information.

   This is a form of control. A Jezebel wields power over you by knowing something you don't know about the situation.

In the eyes of a Jezebel, having information you don't have is a powerful weapon of control.

5. Talks in confusion.

It is impossible to converse with a Jezebel in logic. One pastor wrote a six-page letter to his elders about a situation in the church. The context was so vague that no one was without confusion. This is a way to maintain control and domination. When confronting a Jezebel, the subject may be changed five times in one minute. Confusion keeps them undiscovered and unexposed.

6. Volunteers for anything.

A Jezebel volunteers to establish control. He or she seemingly has endless (nervous) energy and eagerly looks for opportunities to be in charge of projects. Although Jezebels will work hard, the motive is never pure, and eventually their secret agenda cannot be hidden.

7. Lies.

A Jezebel lies convincingly. No one can lie better than they can. They can turn on the charm and make you believe blue is red. Jezebels always fool those whom they've just met while those who have been victimized by their tactics stand by helplessly. The fact that Jezebels can look you in the eye and lie just shows how strong this rebellious and recalcitrant spirit is.

8. Ignores people.

A classic ploy of a controller is to ignore you when you disagree with them. This tactic is frequently used by leaders when someone doesn't agree with their plans, and they isolate the person by ignoring them. Some in these situations have been ignored for months, just because they chose not to be a puppet. This puts the person out of the leader's grace and forces them to either "come around" to the leader's way of thinking or be ignored indefinitely. One is not free to disagree with a controller.

9. Criticizes everyone.

This Jezebel trait is also characteristic of a controller. He has to be the one who looks good, so he will quickly and sharply criticize anyone who makes a suggestion or a plan. Even if he likes the plan, he can only criticize it because the idea did not originate from him. Criticizing others elevates the controller in his own mind.

10. One-upmanship.

Those with a Jezebel spirit will always upstage another person. They feel threatened by anyone who dares to steal the limelight or anyone who is a threat to their power and control. If you are with such a person and tell of your accomplishment or victory, you can be assured that the Jezebel will quickly tell of something they have accomplished.

11. Sequesters information.

A Jezebel loves to be in control of information. If there is ever a situation where information is important, they will push to be the "first" to know it. He or she seems to know everything about everyone. Where they get all their information is beyond comprehension, but they can divulge mass quantities of detailed data about others' lives and actions.

12. Uses information.

Jezebels use information to leverage power and then share tidbits with you, often things told to them in confidence. This gives a Jezebel a sense of power, even to the point of trying to impress people by "knowing things" that others do not.

13. Talks incessantly.

Many people talk habitually, but a Jezebel uses talking as a form of control. In a typical conversation, they do all the talking, whether it is about sports, the weather, or the Kingdom of God. Because of this form of control, Jezebels are unable to receive input from anyone in their life. All conversation with them is one-sided. You are doing the listening.

14. Is pushy and domineering.

A person with a Jezebel spirit pressures you to do things, seemingly ripping from you your right to choose or make a decision for yourself. He or she makes others feel as though they don't have enough sense to think for themselves.

15. Commands attention.

A Jezebel likes to be the center of attention and doesn't like to see others recognized and lauded. When someone else is recognized, the Jezebel will quickly undermine the person's accomplishments verbally.

16. Is vengeful.

Since a Jezebel is never wrong, if you contradict or confront one, get ready to become his or her worst enemy. As long as you are in agreement with the Jezebel, all is fine. But if you confront or challenge him or her, then look out. You are the target of their fiercest venom. A Jezebel will stop at nothing to destroy your reputation.

17. Attempts to make you look like *you're* the Jezebel.

A Jezebel spirit is difficult to pin down. If they are near to being confronted about their actions, they will skillfully twist the entire situation, trying to make the innocent person look like the one who is attempting to control. As always, the Jezebel will do anything to look like the one who is right.

18. Insinuates disapproval.

A Jezebel will often imply disapproval to those under his or her control. The controlled person feels no freedom to express an opinion, for fear of disapproval. This often manifests in a marriage or in a working environment.

19. Is ambitious.

The Jezebel has strong desire, but all for self. "I want what I want when I want it" describes his worship of self-will. A Jezebel leader will never use the words "We have a vision," but rather, "My vision is thus."

20. Gift-giving.

Gift-giving is a form of manipulation a Jezebel uses that always makes you feel obligated to him or her. It also compromises the victim's ability to speak direct, confronting truth. Naturally, not everyone who gives gifts is guilty of control, but gift-giving is a tactic used by those who have a need to control.

HOW DO YOU STOP A JEZEBEL SPIRIT?

At the beginning of this chapter, we quoted the age-old wisdom of war: know your Enemy!

Being able to identify a Jezebel spirit and stopping it before it does major damage—including the dissolution of your church, which is its ultimate aim—starts by knowing with whom you are dealing.

"You stop this spirit's operation in your life only when you pray and obey what the Holy Spirit says," says Jennifer LeClaire. "When you walk in accordance with the Word of God . . . you will dismantle Jezebel's operation." [18]

Robert Morris cautions that you need to prepare for a long and strenuous struggle. "Jezebel will not depart easily. But with prayer and fasting, you can gain the strength for the long haul." [19]

More bitter than death,
is the woman whose heart is snares and nets . . .
he who pleases God shall escape from her,
but the sinner shall be trapped.
—ECCLESIASTES 7:26

THE ENEMY WANTS YOU

Make no mistake about it; the Enemy's greatest plan is to destroy the family. When the family is strong, the nation is strong. When the family is weak, the nation is weak. If he can disassemble the sacred bond of God's perfect union, then he can take down a nation.

THE 40 DAY PRAYER CHALLENGE   155

Unfortunately, he's done a pretty good job so far.

We can see how the Enemy infiltrates our churches, schools, government, and media. But what must we do to stop him?

We MUST pray!

We have been given the power through the Holy Spirit to slam the door in his face. It's time to pick up the sword of truth and fight the good fight. We cannot wait another day. We need an "army of us" to take back what the Enemy has stolen in the mighty name of Jesus! He has no right to anything of yours. You must know who the Enemy is, and you must know who you are. You are an heir of God's, and through your inheritance, you can claim rights to all that He is and has.

When we pray to the King of Kings and the Lord of Lords, our families and our nation will be saved. Release His supernatural power by *speaking* it, *believing* it, and *expecting* it!

Now if we are children, then we are heirs—
heirs of God and co-heirs with Christ.
—ROMANS 8:17, NIV

CHAPTER 7

HEARING THE VOICE OF GOD

Whether you turn to the right or to the left,
your ears will hear a voice behind you, saying,
"This is the way; walk in it."
—ISAIAH 30:21, NIV

AN AUDIBLE VOICE?

Occasionally someone says, "God told me," which leaves you wondering, *Does God really talk to that person and not to me?*

If God has never *spoken* to you in a clear, firm, *out-loud* voice, don't worry—you're in the same boat as most people. In fact, the majority of those who say they have "heard the Voice" are actually referring to an inner voice. We'll address that in a moment.

But those who *have* heard a distinct, audible Voice say it is unforgettable.

Ask Polly.

Polly: An Urgent Voice Said, "Pray Now!"

My two daughters and I were sitting in our usual spot near the back of the church listening to the assistant pastor's sermon.

Suddenly, as if a cloud formed in front of me—almost like a movie before your eyes—I saw a desert-like land with flat buildings. People were running and shouting. There were others in uniforms.

It confused me like nothing I'd ever seen.

As I stared at the images, a man's voice spoke firmly into my left ear, "If you want to see your son alive again, you need to ask for prayer now!"

I turned quickly to see who was speaking.

There were no men seated near me.

I attempted to process what I saw and heard. The voice had been clear, authoritative, and there was an urgency! It was unmistakably *spoken* into my left ear, not inside my head, as if I was thinking it.

My son Christopher was serving as a US marine in Iraq. *Was this about him?*

Without hesitation I stood up and said, "Excuse me!"

The pastor looked at me, slightly surprised, and said, "Yes?"

"God just spoke to me and I need prayer help . . . prayer for our son . . . I know he's in battle!"

The assistant pastor, somewhat bewildered, said, "Okay," then continued his sermon.

I sat down, embarrassed, thinking, *Oh, no . . . they think I am nuts. They may not want me to come back again.* But I told myself . . . I did what I was asked.

As we were leaving the church, Charlie, a good prayer warrior, came up to me, thanked me for having the courage to *speak up*, and said that he noticed a lot of other prayerful people in the church who immediately put their heads down and began to pray for my son.

I thanked him, and thanked God, for keeping my son safe. I felt a peace that I'd done the right thing—standing up and standing on God's word.

That very unusual experience was heavy on my mind; I continued to think about it—and my son—morning, noon, and night. Then, fourteen days later, Christopher telephoned home. He told of a bad fight they been in with the enemy two weeks earlier.

They had cleared a building, and he was about to step out the door when someone behind him said something "smart" to him. It was odd! That caused him to quickly turn on his heels.

That very second a bullet flew by him!

If he had not stopped and turned, the bullet would have hit him in the side of his body armor, a very vulnerable spot for a soldier—known to, and aimed for, by the enemy.

My son never could establish who spoke to him in that unusual manner, but my husband and I cried—knowing it was God who had gotten our son's attention, keeping him safe.

Christopher and his platoon all came home; a few wounded, but no lives were lost.

We thank God every day for all He does for us, and I especially thank God for those friends in church who prayed with me that day and proved the power of prayer.

I dare not think, *What if I had not been obedient to God? What if I had not listened to that voice?*

It is my hope that this true story will inspire everyone, to trust God and pray!

—POLLY HOOK

Hearing and paying attention to the verbal voice of God was literally life-saving for Polly's son Christopher.

God needed her to act at that very moment. There was no time for Polly to question whether the Voice was just something she was thinking; she needed to be obedient to God by immediately standing up and *speaking* her request.

To get her attention, He spoke firmly, audibly, into her left ear, thereby reducing her likelihood of hesitation and self-doubt.

Generally, when you hear an out-loud directive from God, you are in a critical situation, at a time and place where if you don't act instantly, life will be at stake.

MORE OFTEN GOD SPEAKS THROUGH AN INNER VOICE

The vast majority of times when someone says they "heard a Voice," they're referring to an *inner voice*. It may be a strong instinctive communication or verbalized words—like hearing the lyrics to a song inside your head—but in either case, the communication can be just as forceful and authoritative as the audible voice that Polly experienced.

HUBIE SYNN: YOU MUST TRUST THE "VOICE"

Recently we had a dear friend, Hubie Synn, speak at our church on the subject "Hearing the Voice of God."

He's an accountant who receives strong inner compulsions to approach complete strangers and say, "God has a message for you."

Usually, upon hearing the message, recipients are left with their jaws dropped.

Hubie is called a modern-day prophet, vetted by some of America's most respected ministries, yet he is a *reluctant* prophet. He says he's "scared" to approach strangers because of his innate shyness and fear of looking foolish.

However, should he stall or hesitate in delivering the prophetic word, a different feeling comes over him—nausea. That's when he'll give up his resistance and submit to God's will.

For instance, one day he felt a strong nudge from God to communicate with a man at an airport and give him a message. The stranger looked like he was Jewish and seemed to be praying. Hubie did his typical hesitating. Only when the feeling of nausea began to creep into his stomach did he direct his attention to the man, who was separated by an empty seat.

Patiently waiting until the man acknowledged him, Hubie smiled and said, "God has a message for you." The man nodded and words flowed through Hubie's lips, emanating from a deep inner source, outside of his own control. As he never knows nor remembers what was said, Hubie feels like a bystander as God does the talking. He was later told that he had said the book the man had written would have a major impact.

Because Hubie had no personal knowledge about anything the man may have written, he also had no way of knowing that while he was waiting, the man was asking for God's direction. He was pleading for God to help find him a publisher for the manuscript he had labored over and just completed. Nor could Hubie ever have anticipated that the one publisher Hubie had recently met through another client would turn out to be the ideal publisher for the man's work.

Hubie's prophetic word from God came true. Months later, the man's first book—Jonathan Cahn's blockbuster *The Harbinger*—entered the *New York Times* bestseller list and remained there for more than 120 weeks.

Today, Hubie and his wife, Vicki, attend Jonathan Cahn's church, the largest Messianic church in America.

On another occasion, the distinct feeling came over Hubie to give a new client—a New York Giants football player—a "word from the Lord." [1]

Again Hubie wrestled with the decision to call the man, possibly offending him—at the least, causing embarrassment, or worse, losing the client altogether.

As a nauseous feeling arouse in his stomach, Hubie acquiesced to God's nudging, telephoned the man, David Tyree, and said, in essence, "God wants you to know that He is going to give you the platform you have desired to talk about the Gospel."

On the other end of the phone Tyree was quiet, then confessed that he and his wife had just been praying about that, feeling that perhaps his career was waning due to a sluggish season and injuries, and that he may never achieve the visibility he'd desired from his NFL career in order to ignite his post-football dream to spread the Gospel.

Some five months later, Hubie and his wife watched as the New York Giants were the underdogs in the 2008 Super Bowl against the highly favored New England Patriots. The Giants were behind with only one minute and fifteen seconds left to play. David Tyree was dashing down the field as Eli Manning dodged several tacklers and threw a desperate pass. [2]

David rose in the air in sync with the Patriots' best defender. In a collision of muscle and grit, David caught the ball by holding it to his helmet. The Giants won the game on the next play, and ESPN labeled David's "helmet catch" as the "greatest catch in Super Bowl history!"

With that, David's prayer—and Hubie's prophecy—came true: David Tyree shall forever have a "platform" to talk about God.

Hubie Synn has learned to understand the clear "nudgings" that God gives him to speak with complete strangers and others, and feels that it's more like a partnership with God. As with any partner with whom you have a close personal relationship and work with every day, Hubie says, "I talk to God all the time."

In other words, Hubie prays all the time.

Yet isn't that like any wonderful relationship you may have with a friend, a sister, your parents, your boss? The more you communicate in a meaningful manner, the better your relationship?

Hubie once contended that Louise "has some of what I have": that she receives prophetic messages from the Lord, but that she needs to increase her trust in God that they indeed are from Him.

In fact, there are several occasions on which God has spoken with her profoundly, yet for Louise, "hearing the Voice of God" was neither an audible voice nor an inaudible one inside her head. Instead, "It's like a ticker tape going across my chest," she says.

Louise
WHEN GOD'S "VOICE" IS A TICKER TAPE

Hubie's words were resonating with me as SQuire and I boarded a plane for a five-hour flight to Los Angeles.

Shortly after takeoff, a baby began to cry. Not just fussing and whimpering—this tiny tot was wailing at the top of her lungs. It got to the point where it had been going on for two hours!

Passengers were losing patience, and the mother's anguish became increasingly evident as she continued to walk up and down the aisle, patting and bouncing the baby, trying to calm her down.

I rose from my seat to use the restroom. While I was in there, I had an overwhelming sense—like a ticker tape across my chest—that God was asking me to lay hands on the baby, to *speak* prayers for her, and if I did, she would stop crying.

I quickly dismissed the feeling. But it got stronger by the second.

Inside my head I argued with God: *I can't just go up to a woman I don't know and lay hands on her baby! She might get angry. She might be scared I'm trying to hurt her baby. She might try to have me arrested!*

As I exited the restroom, wouldn't you know, the mother and her crying baby were right there, in a seat just outside the door!

Oh, great, I thought. *Now what am I going to do?*

I smiled at the mother and somewhat awkwardly said, "I'm just going to pray for your baby."

I was too self-conscious to remember whether I *spoke* the prayer out loud or in silence, but the second I touched that baby, she stopped crying!

The mother didn't say a word, and I wasn't about to hang around to see what she had to say, so I quickly went back to my seat.

I felt a peace come over me. I had been obedient to God.

In retrospect I wondered: *Was that an action-step of faith intended for me . . . or for the mother and her baby?* Whatever the reason, I'm sure the passengers were happy, since the baby slept the rest of the way to Los Angeles.

At my seat I picked up the book I had been reading, which was called *How to Pray* by R. A. Torrey.

How ironic, I thought. Then, as I continued reading, a white feather floated down from above and landed on my sleeve.

I looked up. None of the bulkheads was open, causing me to wonder how that feather could have appeared out of thin air.

I looked at SQuire and pointed to the feather, smiling like it was a mysterious prank. I took the opportunity to whisper to him what I felt God had told me to say to the frazzled mom, for he, I'm sure, had noted that the child was no longer screaming.

"That's a godwink!" he said, puzzling me for a moment. "I was just writing about feathers on my posting."

He showed me his Godwink Gathering page on Facebook where he'd just quoted someone who said that feathers are signs of angelic visitations.

I smiled with satisfaction, acknowledging that God was confirming with a godwink that He had certainly spoken to me, and most important, that I had listened.

It reminded me of another discussion I'd had with Hubie. He told me that when you "hear the voice of God," you have to go out on a limb and test the waters. God will meet you, take you by the hand, and guide you. Even though I was nervous, I had taken that first step and it felt good, because God was there.

FIVE WAYS TO KNOW IT'S GOD SPEAKING TO YOU

1. **Faith is present.**
   The Bible says that "Faith comes from hearing the message, and the message is heard through the word about Christ." [3]

2. **God's message always agrees with Scripture.**
   God will not tell you to do something that does not align with His Word.

3. **God usually confirms His message with a sign—a godwink.**

Polly, for example, got a confirmation that she had indeed heard God's urgent warning when she received the call from her son two weeks later and he recounted the perilous situation that he had been in, at the very moment she was instructed by the Voice to ask for prayer. And Louise had a godwink about the feather.

4. **God's message often arrives during prayer.**

If you are in the midst of prayer, you can be pretty well assured that a brilliant idea you just received was a message from Him. On other occasions, God will place someone on your heart while you are praying, and when you call that person, you often learn that God needed for you to reach out to them.

5. **The inner feeling grows stronger with time.**

When God is trying to speak with you, thoughts and ideas begin to resonate and grow. His Voice may be like a nudge or a tap on your shoulder that doesn't go away.

My sheep hear My voice, and I know them,
and they follow Me.
—John 10:27, ESV

Perhaps the most frequent "Voice from God" that people encounter is through a deep, highly compelling *instinct* that you *know* must have been from Him because of its intensity.

Haven't you stood on a curb, about to step off, when something inexplicable inside stops you, pulls you back, just in time to miss a truck or a car whooshing by?

Or as a mother, have you ever had an overwhelming inner urge to check on your child?

THE VOICE ONLY A MOTHER HEARS

The inner voice of God, as a supernatural transmission, seems to be particularly directed to the internal receivers of mothers. Not that men aren't also the recipients of life-changing communications from a "still small voice within,"[4] but particularly when it comes to their children, the experiences of mothers provide exceptional evidence of divine intervention.

Our daily Godwink Gathering on Facebook[5] offers a platform to more than a quarter of a million people around the globe to share their godwink experiences. We never cease to be amazed by the number of stories told by mothers who have received clear, concise directives with immediacy, which they later believed was the Voice of God. Following are just a few of those letters:

WHEN YOU HEAR THE VOICE . . . ACTION IS NECESSARY

My daughter was just two months old and I put her to bed for the night. She lay fast asleep when I closed the door. I was not scheduled to check on her again until her 4:00 a.m. feeding.

Within ten minutes I was halted in my tracks by a Voice commanding . . . "Check on her NOW!"

Although I was alone, the Voice did not frighten me. I immediately obeyed.

When I opened her door, I was shocked to see that the
elastic stitching had unraveled from the bumper guards and was
wrapped around her neck and she was turning blue!

Had I not heeded that Voice—that I know to have been from
God—my daughter would not have lived.

—JT[6]

The Voice Speaks with No Time to Spare

I have had the nudge many times. My sons and I were hiking at
Crabtree Falls. They ran off the path to the water, and I stayed
on the path watching them.

I got a feeling to leave NOW! So I called the boys to come
back—we needed to go.

Like most kids, they complained, and I called them several
times and, as the feeling got stronger, I yelled very loudly. They
came running up the hill.

As we retreated along the path, we heard a loud crash!

A huge tree fell right where they had been playing! If I
had not listened to the nudge, I may have lost my boys that
day.

—DW[7]

When God Tells You Something Only He Would Know

When my son was eighteen months old, they heard a defec-
tive sound in his heart.

I was holding his crying, trembling, scared little body as we took him into radiology. I said I would hold him to get him through the X-rays.

But, as clear as could be . . . I heard God's Voice.

"You cannot go in with him—you are pregnant!"

This was news to me!

But, trusting the Voice that I had never before heard, I obeyed, and allowed my son to go through the procedure without me. He did just fine. But two weeks later, it was confirmed. I *was* pregnant!

—SA[8]

WHEN YOU ARE RESCUED BY THE VOICE

When I was little, my mom woke up, telling everyone the house was on fire and to get out! She was frantic, saying a Voice had awakened her from sleep and told her the house was on fire.

She ignored the Voice at first. Then it repeated the same thing with more urgency.

No one believed her because there was no sign of fire or smoke anywhere, but when we went outside, the top of the house was in flames.

If it hadn't been for the Voice warning us, my family of nine would probably not be here.

—BLS[9]

The Voice Speaks with Urgency!

I was taking care of my nephew and niece outside my aunt's house. They were riding up and down the short driveway beside her house.

I distinctly heard in my head: "MOVE THE CHILDREN NOW!"

So I moved them to the front yard.

Just then, a man got into a car across the street, backed up, and zoomed directly into my aunt's driveway, right where the kids had been playing only a minute or so before!

—Kim[10]

I will listen to what the Lord says.
—Psalms 85:8, NIV

When the next letter arrived from a mother who had heard the Voice, we paused; should we post it or not? After praying about it, we determined that the Godwink Gathering audience should have an opportunity to express their own feelings. You'll hear the outcome after you read the letter.

A Mother's Torment for Ignoring the Voice

I heard the Voice telling me, "Go home!"

I called home, where my three sons were supposed to be, but no one answered. Assuming they were playing outside, I decided to remain at my best friend's house.

At about 4:00 p.m., my friend's phone rang. I answered, but no one was on the other end.

The Voice inside me—a strong male voice inside my head—became louder, "GO HOME!"

But, in my rational mind, I determined that the Voice was irrational. So again, I ignored it.

An hour later the phone rang once more. This time it was the call that forever changed my world.

My twelve-year-old son was screaming that Aaron, my eighteen-year-old son, had hanged himself!

Every day I live with the guilt for not listening to the Voice. The price paid was my precious son's life.

It's coming up on fifteen years, but the pain of losing Aaron never goes away, and the thought that *"If only I'd listened to that voice, he would still be here"* torments my soul.

—Alisha Gilman[11]

Alisha's heartfelt letter was posted[12] on Godwink Gathering. A total of 250,536 people responded. Most were other mothers reaching out to assure Alisha that they did not believe God was holding her accountable and that indeed her courage in posting her story on Godwink Gathering was of service to many of them who had questioned the Voice when they themselves had heard it.

As the seventeenth anniversary of her son's loss recently approached, we spoke with Alisha about her torment just after the tragedy.

"I pushed away from God for a long while," said Alisha.

She questioned God for six months—why He allowed it to happen—why He failed to intervene when He surely must have known that she had misunderstood His Voice. She heard of another child on the brink of shooting himself, and God sent an angel to push the gun away at the last moment. Where was God when *she* needed Him?

"Where *are* you, God?" she cried, her words wrapped in anguish.

Suddenly she felt something strange.

"A warm feeling like oil came over me and answered my question."

It was not the authoritative-male-inside-your-head Voice she'd heard that terrible day, but a strong inner sense.

It said, "I'm right here. As I was the day I lost *my* son."

That day marked the beginning of Alisha's healing. She began to understand that "I'm never going to get through this without God."

Today Alisha says, "I'm back in love with Jesus." Hindsight allows her to see how her life has changed. "My loss opened my eyes to other people's pain. It's a rare person who hasn't suffered a loss of some sort. If telling my story can help just one person—one mother who is doubting the Voice of God—please tell it."

It's a comfort to know that God does not blame Alisha. He loves each of us completely and purely. His word assures that there is no condemnation in Him.

> *There is now no condemnation*
> *for those who are in Christ Jesus.*
> —ROMANS 8:1, NIV

Feelings of guilt and shame don't come from God. Satan tried to use Aaron's tragedy to destroy Alisha's life. But she allowed God to heal her heart, to ease the pain, and He, in turn, has given her the gift of empathy to help others who have suffered similarly.

WHAT IF I STILL HAVEN'T HEARD THE VOICE OF GOD?

Just because you haven't heard from God—from inside or outside your head—does not mean He's not communicating with you. God is always trying to connect with you, in multiple ways, every day.

When you open your senses to allow him in, you can see God's existence all around you. His voice in the trill of a blackbird, His fragrance in the petals of a rose, His grace in an unexpected godwink.

SQuire
FINDING HIM IN THE GODWINKS OF YOUR LIFE

As mentioned in chapter 1, godwinks are those little "so-called coincidences that you know aren't coincidence." They are person-to-person messages, directly to you, and so extraordinary that you know they must be of divine origin.

When you take a moment to pull back the lens of your life and marvel at the amazing connections that have caused you to be in precisely the right place at the right time, you'll see that you have already experienced godwinks—a form of God's voice to you. Perhaps you were introduced to a new job that opened exciting vistas; experienced a relationship that blossomed into love and marriage; or encountered someone who led you to unknown information or beliefs that altered the quality of your life. In each case, God's voice was *speaking* to you through godwinks.

And just to harp on this point, how do you get more godwinks in order to hear His Voice more frequently? You pray.

When you pray, godwinks happen because of the second meaning for godwinks, which I addressed earlier: "Answered prayer." Let your requests be known to God, He listens, and His replies are often delivered via godwinks.

A CHECKLIST ON HEARING THE VOICE OF GOD

1. **If you hear an audible Voice,** it is likely to be firm, pithy, and urgent, as it was with Polly.
2. **An inner Voice speaking to you**—the most frequent experience—may be hearing words inside your head like the lyrics to a song. It's important to pay attention!
3. **Talk with God all the time.** Continuous prayer creates a strong relationship between you and your Father, through which you are more likely to be paying attention when He speaks back to you, as Hubie Synn has learned.
4. **Be obedient to the Voice.** Bravely step out in faith as Louise did to pray for the crying child and God will often give you a sign of confirmation.
5. **Acknowledge godwinks** as nonverbal voices from God, usually provided as messages of confirmation or reassurance. As

you acknowledge and allow your godwinks, they will seem to multiply.

The Voice of God does indeed speak to you at all times, and if you're listening, you can hear Him. Whether it's a warning or a message of comfort, He wants to be in frequent prayerful communication with you.

He who has an ear, let him hear
what the Spirit says.
—REVELATION 3:22, NIV

CHAPTER 8

GROWING IN YOUR PRAYER TOGETHER

CONGRATULATIONS!

If you have been taking The 40 Day Prayer Challenge as part of this book, you have now completed six weeks—or forty days—of praying together with your partner. Your first order of business is to log on to **PrayStay.org** and take the second Baylor University survey. You will then be able to download a report displaying your personal progress in all areas of your relationship.

Using the unique login and password you used on the first survey, you can now sign in on separate devices. You will be able to see bar graphs of how well you and your partner did.

WHAT'S NEXT?

If you have faithfully prayed together for forty days, we are certain you have experienced exactly what God promised—you have witnessed extraordinary outcomes in your relationship and in all aspects of your lives. The truth of the scriptures has come alive for you; that "when two or more are gathered together in His name," He has been there among you. Are we right?

Be that the case . . . here's the big question: why would you
stop praying together?

If this time of daily prayer is so incredible, why would you
not want to keep it going as a part of your daily routine, building
upon the joys you've experienced?

This is the time that you can take this wonderful sense of oneness with God and allow the relationship that you and your partner are feeling right now to mature—three cords wound tightly
together that can never be broken.

IS IT TIME FOR POSTGRADUATE WORK?

As an enthusiastic advocate for consistent prayer by two people,
perhaps it's time to share your gift from God. You can help orga-
nize or lead small group meetings that introduce the joy of couples, family members, or friends praying together.

Kenny and Donna McLeod lead many small groups at the
Church of the Highlands in Birmingham and help train other
small-group leaders and coaches.

"One of the most important principles that we have discovered," says Kenny, "is that God has given us a gift that we are to
give away!" [1]

"God wants to use your story," adds Donna, and He can do
that exponentially with the multiplication of small groups that
undertake The 40 Day Prayer Challenge.

See if your church can start The 40 Day Prayer Challenge,
either with the entire congregation or in small groups. Find out
more at PrayStay.org.

Like Kenny and Donna, when you become a part of the testimonies of others, witnessing the ways in which marriages, re-

lationships, families, and friendships are becoming empowered by Partnered Prayer, you'll feel spiritual rewards that are beyond measure.

> *Do not be anxious about anything, but in every situation,*
> *by prayer and petition, with thanksgiving,*
> *present your requests to God.*
> —Philippians 4:6, NIV

Reflecting on the Promises in This Book

At the beginning, we predicted that this book "will show you how *speaking* words of prayer, in faith, will plug you into the greatest power strip in the universe."

Story after story has supported the premise that you have astonishing power in your lips—power to tap into the grid of spiritual energy that comes directly from God and to feel your own life changing from sadness to joy, from unhealthy to healthy, from uncertain to certain.

You can see how those around you begin to change as well. Several couples have told similar stories; that a few weeks into The 40 Day Prayer Challenge, their children asked, "What happened to you and Mom?" or ". . . to you and Dad?"

Kids are always much more perceptive and "tuned in" than we think. They may look like they're absorbed in other things, but they notice "something is different" when their mothers and fathers are now three-as-one with God.

When you and your prayer partner accept the promise Christ gives you in Matthew 21:22, that "whatever you ask in prayer, if you believe, you will receive"[2]—adopting the personal commitment to *speak* it, *believe* it, and *expect* it—your entire existence takes on new clarity and becomes altered for the better.

For the remaining time we have together in this book, let's reflect on some points that exemplify that.

FROM CHAPTER 1: WHEN PASTORS PRAY WITH SPOUSES

In chapter 1, we heard Pastor Jeff Winter confess, "Yikes, I'm a pastor and I rarely pray with my wife." Jeff and Judy rediscovered a joy in their marriage that seemed to have been stored away somewhere for years. As a bonus, God answered their prayers to bring their son back to the Lord.

Pastor Tim Keller admitted reluctance and guilt when his wife, Kathy, asked him "to pray with her every night." Her simple line of reasoning left him speechless: "Imagine you were diagnosed with a lethal condition and the doctor told you that you would die unless you took a particular pill every night. Would you not get around to it some nights? No, you would never miss."

They began to pray together, every night, and haven't stopped for thirteen years.

In that same chapter, two British researchers melded the results of sixteen hundred studies on the role of faith and health. The salient outcome: people who have faith live seven years longer.

FROM CHAPTER 2: WHAT WE LEARNED ABOUT WORDS

We told you the story of composer Al Kasha, whose number one hit recording for "The Morning After" had just been honored with an Academy Award. Yet despite that success, he was gripped with fear, trapped in the imprisonment of agoraphobia, afraid to leave the house.

That is *what* happened. This is *why* it happened.

For years Al's fears and phobias were bubbling beneath the surface like a long-dormant volcano. One day the *negative* words spoken to him long ago by his angry, drunken father erupted in fear, rendering him panicked and immobilized for years. He remained that way until the *negative* words of his earthly father were preempted by the *positive* promise of his Heavenly Father via a middle-of-the-night television voice saying, "God's perfect love casts out all fear."

Because those were God's words directly from the Bible, *spoken* in a commanding manner, they took on a life of their own!

Recall that Proverbs says, "Death and life are in the power of the tongue." [3]

The speaker, Robert Schuller, truly *believed* that God *could* cast out all fear, and had an *expectation* that those words would pierce into the dark of night to divinely connect with someone whom God had intended. That person was Al Kasha.

If words of discouragement were able to sear into the memory of a highly successful man, imagine how the power of your words impacts your children, your marriage, or your relationships.

Words can be weapons that tear down the human spirit, leaving wounds deeper than a physical beating.

But words are also tools we can use to build love, hope, and character.

Compare Al Kasha's childhood experiences with those of Roy Eaton, a poor kid who grew up to become the first black man to break the white barrier on Madison Avenue. Words became his tools in advertising. Among other things, Eaton wrote the Texaco copy line "You can trust your car to the man who wears the star."[4]

The words spoken by Eaton's mother as he left for school fueled his belief beyond his circumstances. "You must always do two hundred percent to get credit for one hundred percent," she would remind him.[5]

A single idea about hard work, conveyed by the words of a loving parent, can produce huge returns in the life of a child.

By the same token, when you redundantly speak the Word of God, as good fruit, into your child's life, it will take root. As Jesus said, "The seed is the word of God."[6]

Do you remember something that was said to you as a young person, by a respected adult, that stayed with you for a long while?

SQuire

I can recall a scene in the fall of eighth grade, on the junior varsity football field, some distance from where Coach Rector was working out the more important varsity team. My physical build was smaller than most, but I made up for it in scrappy enthusiasm. On this particular day, I got lucky. I made a tackle around the shoestrings of a big guy carrying the ball and brought him down.

"Rushnel-l-l-l!"

I heard my name echo over the field as everything came to a halt. My teammates and I stood waiting, in our droopy, oversized uniforms, watching the coach approach in a determined stride from the adjacent field.

Did I do something wrong? I wondered.

"Rushnel-l-l-l . . . great tackle."

Imagine that! The coach had spotted my tackle from the distance of a football field away and came all that way to articulate that encouragement.

Many decades later, I can still hear those words echoing in my memory. Three simple words—"Rushnell, great tackle." They fueled my spirits for years.

LITTLE MINDS ARE GREATLY INFLUENCED BY THE TALK OF ADULTS

Dr. Norman Vincent Peale, author of *The Power of Positive Thinking,* once shared a research study with which his ministry had been involved. It demonstrated that in kindergarten, children tend to be positive thinkers, but by the time they are only two years older, they become more and more negative in their outlook, taking on the attitudes of adults around them.[7]

That pleases the Enemy. He loves to start planting seeds of doubt and fear into moldable young minds. These grow to become huge burdens by adolescence and heavy baggage in adulthood.

We each have an opportunity to be in God's service to counter that. As mothers, fathers, aunts, uncles, grandparents, and neighbors, we are in a unique position to help young people to "put on the full armor of God" so that they are protected throughout life. We need to help them suit up against all the destructive, hurtful, and negative words that can pollute their little minds, by giving them affirmative, positive, and Godly statements that will gird them up.

THE DIFFERENCE BETWEEN POSITIVE THINKING AND FAITH THINKING

As Dr. Peale has taught, it is of great benefit to live your life with an attitude of positive thinking. But Dr. Peale would be the first to tell you that there's a significant difference between your positive attitude and your faith attitude. A positive attitude comes from man—you or the people around you—while a faith attitude comes from God.

Jesus didn't command you to think "positive" thoughts about getting rid of that mountain you're facing—which could be fear, betrayal, addiction, or debt. He said for you to *speak* to that mountainous problem and with a firm attitude of faith, that it *will* be moved—a deep *belief* that it will be gone—and to *expect* the outcome you have asked for.

You must expel any doubt by learning to replace doubt with faith instantly.

Doubt is human conditioning. Faith is God conditioning. As the scriptures tell us, let our minds rest not "on human wisdom, but on God's power." [8]

WHAT ABOUT THE WORDS YOU SPEAK TO YOURSELF?

If you feel you're lacking God's blessings in your life, perhaps the words you're saying to *yourself* are blocking the steady flow of His goodness. Your negative words will put a crimp in the hose carrying God's goodness, thereby causing the flow from the source to slow to a trickle.

When someone asks, "How are you doing?" do you find yourself saying, "Well, I'm doing all right, under the circumstances"?

God doesn't want you to live your life according to your circumstances. He has called you to live *over* and *through* the circumstances you see before you. He wants you to "live by faith, not by sight." [9]

If you find yourself telling folks "I guess I was just lucky" when good fortune occurs, please think about this. The word *lucky* is never mentioned in the Bible. Instead, you'll find an abundance of promises that God's blessings are just waiting to burst into your life. In Romans 8:28, for instance, He promises that "all things will work together for good." That means all the bad things and all the good things that happen to you will work together for good.

Your faith will be increased when you understand the truth of the scripture. "For with God, nothing shall be impossible." [10]

*Faith isn't the ability to believe long and far into
the misty future. It's simply taking God at his word
and taking the next step.*
—JONI EARECKSON TADA

FROM CHAPTER 3: WISDOM FROM COUPLES, FAMILIES, AND FRIENDS

In this chapter, Leslie said she just wanted Erick to "put his arms around me and pray *for* me . . . and *with* me." On week four of The 40 Day Prayer Challenge she was overjoyed when he "moved from the kitchen table to the couch." Then, as he prayed aloud for the first time, "tears streamed down my cheeks."

Pam wrote, "almost everyone thought Jay and I had it all together . . . we knew we didn't have it together." Then, after a few weeks of praying together, "we were the topic of quite a few conversations about the change people could see in us."

We learned the lifelong impact of answered prayer on a twelve-year-old boy, Tim Conway. Even today the famous comedian looks back on the day that God confirmed His presence. Tim had prayed for the ability to hook one particular duck from sixty that were bobbing in a carnival tank of water. His prayer was answered and he got the prize: a cross on a green ribbon that glowed in the dark. The little boy in Tim Conway kept it under his pillow long after college.

Pauletta Washington said that "the snapshot of seeing your parents praying together is a priceless treasure to pass along to your children."

Karen Covell, discussing how prayer was a vital part of the family fabric as she and Jim raised two boys, says that "prayer is not preparation for the greater work, prayer IS the greater work."

The two praying friends, Dee and Gloria, jotted a memorable quote into their prayer journal. Said Gloria, "I was given a choice of fear or faith. I chose to walk by faith through the fire."

FROM CHAPTER 4: CHURCHES PRAYING TOGETHER

We heard four incredible stories about the awesome power that descends from Heaven when the congregations of churches lock arms and cry out in prayer.

How the journey of Jim Cymbala's Brooklyn Tabernacle

Church began with the "C-r-r-rack" of a broken pew, collapsing in a cloud of dust, throwing five parishioners to the floor.

When the pastor literally cried out for prayer, with tears rolling down his cheeks, the small attendance of twenty or so pledged to engage the Lord in regular prayer. Today their Tuesday night prayer meeting is generally attended by three thousand or more, as the church's membership has expanded to some sixteen thousand. Recently the 280-voice Brooklyn Tabernacle Choir sang at a presidential inauguration.

In another story, the small yet prayer-filled Beacon of Hope Church on Martha's Vineyard organized an energetic prayer effort for one of its own, Peter Vincent.

After twice dying of a heart attack on his vacation in the Dominican Republic, Peter came back to life. Prayer worked! A few weeks later the congregation gave him a standing ovation as he walked into church on his own, with only the help of a cane.

Fourteen-year-old John Smith fell into the ice-cold lake and was dead for nearly an hour. He was returned to life, explained one doctor, "when his heart was jump-started by the Holy Spirit listening to the request of a praying mother." A vast prayer vigil by his church resulted in John Smith walking out of the hospital sixteen days after he was submerged. He had no brain, lung, or eye damage; in fact, no damage whatsoever.

The final testimony praising the support of a praying church was the Tom Renfro story. Diagnosed with stage-four lymphoma cancer, with zero prospects of hope, Tom's church and community arranged twelve-hour-a-day prayer chains for forty days. When there was still no hope at the end of forty days, they started again.

Tumors the size of baseballs grotesquely popped up all over his body, bulging from his neck, chest, and abdomen. In a last-ditch effort to keep Tom alive just a few weeks longer until Christmas, he was scheduled for chemotherapy. Yet just before the chemo began, the church's prayers were answered! One by one, the tumors disappeared! Two weeks later Tom stood in tears before his congregation at church, thanking them for the miracle that their prayers had produced.

FROM CHAPTER 5: A NATION IN PRAYER

Benjamin Franklin implored the Continental Congress to turn to prayer to break the impasse that had lasted for weeks.

"God governs in the affairs of men," said the statesman, "and if a sparrow cannot fall to the ground without his notice, is it probable that an empire can rise without his aid?"

The motion to pray didn't pass a vote, but something happened; the representatives must have prayed together privately, for within hours the impasse was lifted.

George Washington exemplified the power of prayer when he became the only officer astride a horse in a battle in Pennsylvania who wasn't wounded despite four bullet holes in his coat. All remaining eighty-six officers were casualties.

Dwight D. Eisenhower probably would never have been president had his family not fervently prayed that he be healed from a wounded, infected leg that doctors wanted to amputate but were prevented from doing so by Ike and his brother.

FROM CHAPTER 6: GETTING TO KNOW YOUR ENEMY

"If you know neither the enemy nor yourself, you will succumb in every battle," wrote military expert Sun Tzu, five hundred years before Christ. His counsel has been followed by generals in successful battles ever since.

In this chapter we learned that the Enemy is there waiting for you. Therefore, arming yourself in prayer and the scriptures is vital to your survival. Yet "most of the power the Enemy ever has is what you give him."

FROM CHAPTER 7: LEARNING TO HEAR THE VOICE OF GOD

"I believe everyone can hear the Voice of God," says Hubie Synn, an accountant who is also a remarkable modern-day prophet. The key, he believes, is to talk with God all the time; then God will begin to talk with you.

In this chapter we learned that there are many ways for us to "hear" God's voice. Sometimes people hear an audible voice outside their heads or, more frequently, sense a voice in the same way you "hear" a song inside your head.

Many mothers shared testimonies of an urgent voice telling them to check on their children. But the most heartfelt was the story of Alisha: "Every day I live with the guilt for not listening to the Voice. The price paid was my precious son's life." Today Alisha works with other parents to encourage them to listen to the Voice.

Another way to experience the Voice of God is to allow godwinks to unfold.

SQuire
EVIDENCE OF GODWINKS: PRAYERS ANSWERED

In chapter 1 we pointed out that "when you pray, godwinks happen," and that this new word, *godwink*, has become an alternative expression for people who are referencing "answered prayer."

To firmly establish this concept for you, may we end this book with one of the most amazing godwink stories I've had the opportunity to write. Nearly every story is astonishing to some degree, but this one takes the prize for the *most* astonishing of all. This is about Toni and David Espinoza's answered prayer, which was first told in my book *Divine Alignment: How Godwink Moments Guide Your Journey*. Toni's fervent prayer was answered with not just one godwink that defied extraordinary mathematical odds, but two.

TONI AND DAVID: ONE OF THE MOST AMAZING GODWINKS

Toni's husband, David, was diagnosed with congestive heart failure in his early fifties. Three separate doctors gave him a matter of months to live unless he received a heart transplant.

Toni and David live in McAllen, Texas, one of the southernmost cities, right on the Mexican border. It was a five-hour drive up to Houston, where they scheduled an appointment with specialists at the DeBakey Heart Institute.

Further confirming their grim prospects, the Houston doctors advised that finding a suitable donor would be tricky, and it may take nine months or so.

Returning home, Toni rallied everyone in the family, in the

neighborhood, and at their church to pray that her husband's life would be saved and that God would quickly lead them to the perfect donor.

Yet as her prayers were *spoken*, Toni became conflicted. It didn't seem right that someone had to die so David could live. So she altered course. She decided to ask God for a complete healing of David so that a heart transplant would not be needed.

As they approached early December that year, Toni's faith was deepening; she sensed that God would answer her prayer. But . . . just to give her comfort . . . she asked Him for a sign. She asked God to confirm that David would be healed by making it snow in McAllen, Texas, on Christmas Day.

She mentioned her prayer to a friend whom she'd known for years, Crawford Higgins.

He looked at her seriously. "Toni, you've lived here most of your life, right?"

She nodded.

"Have you ever *seen* snow?"

She slowly shook her head.

"Do you know that it hasn't snowed in McAllen in one hundred and nine years—and never on Christmas?"

Toni smiled. She was resolved in her faith.

At home later that day, she kept right on *speaking* and *believing* her dual prayer—that David would be healed and that his miracle-to-be would be confirmed by a weather phenomenon unprecedented in the history of McAllen, Texas.

Have you observed that God is never late, rarely early, and almost always right on time?

At 11:45 p.m. on Christmas Eve, the people of McAllen, Texas, were startled to see snow falling for the first time in their lives!

Toni slid open the screen door to the backyard, stepped out, and marveled at the falling snow; it covered the roses in full bloom, speckled her hair and face, mixing with the tears flowing from her eyes.

"Thank you, God. Thank you. Thank you."

The snow meant one thing: it was her sign that David was soon going to celebrate her primary prayer—her *expectant* belief that he would be healed.

She couldn't wait for his regularly scheduled appointment at DeBakey Heart Institute a few days into January.

That Christmas morning McAllen children were bundled up and sent outside to make fan angels and snowmen.

The newspaper ran a special edition with a gala headline: "First White Christmas Ever."

No one ever knew, not even the bishop of her church, that Toni's unshakable faith was directly related to the weather phenomenon. Her story was not revealed until we were able to tell it.

As they waited for Dr. Guillermo Torre to enter the office, Toni and David sat quietly.

He carried papers with him, sat down, stared at the report, looked at the name, looked at David, asked him to confirm his name, and then, with astonishment, said, "I can't explain this. But, David, you're going to be around for a long time."

David Espinoza was given a new lease on life.

Sweet Toni Espinoza was given a powerful affirmation that God really does listen! When she cried out; *speaking* it, firmly *believing* it; and *expecting* it . . . she simply *knew* God would answer. He did—with two amazing godwinks that defy all human odds.

If Toni's prayers were answered, and David lived, why can't yours be answered?

We can all see God in exceptional things, but it requires
the growth of spiritual discipline to see God in every detail.
Never believe that the so-called random events of life are any-
thing less than God's appointed order. Be ready to discover
His divine designs anywhere and everywhere.[11]
—OSWALD CHAMBERS

OUR HOPE FOR YOU

We sincerely hope that you have been blessed and inspired by
the many personal testimonies shared in this book. We hope you
will agree that the evidence is indisputable; God is your protector,
comforter, forgiver, deliverer, rescuer, healer, counselor, liberator,
redeemer, restorer, and so much more.

The Divine Designer who holds and counts every star in the
sky also catches every tear you shed. He is intimately concerned
with every aspect of your life and loves you totally and unconditionally.

Look up into the heavens. Who created all the stars?
He brings them out like an army, one after another,
calling each by its name. Because of his great power
and incomparable strength, not a single one is missing.
—ISAIAH 40:26, NLV

Today is a great day to encourage others to make a commitment to take The 40 Day Prayer Challenge. We can boldly guar-
antee that when you come before the throne of God every day,

192 SQUIRE RUSHNELL AND LOUISE DUART

it will become one of the most treasured times of your day and your life.

God never said "if" you pray; He said "when" you pray.

He, therefore, expects you to be obedient so that He can bless you exceedingly and abundantly. When you give Him time in prayer, God sets things in motion. There is a thin veil that separates heaven and earth, and when you pray passionately and persistently, God will lift the veil and pour down blessings beyond measure.

Give, and it will be given to you.
A good measure, pressed down, shaken together
and running over, will be poured into your lap.
—LUKE 6:38, NIV

God has sent you an invitation with an RSVP on it. Will you accept His invitation to continue to pray to Him? Will you enter into Partnered Prayer with the love of your life, your family member, or your friend every day?

Christ is knocking at the door to your heart!

Here I am! I stand at the door and knock.
If anyone hears my voice and opens the door,
I will come in and eat with him, and he with me.
—REVELATION 3:20, NIV

STUDY GUIDE

SESSION #1

The four discussion segments typically have four questions to stimulate conversation. It's up to the group leader to decide whether to go through all the questions before moving on.

GROUP LEADER

What if you were given a key that would unlock the door to the most powerful force in the universe? Would you use it?

That key is available to you right now. It is called PRAYER!

Jesus promises us the key in Matthew 21:22, "Whatever you ask in prayer . . . if you believe . . . you will receive." [1]

He didn't say *some* of what you ask in prayer . . . you *might* receive. He was very specific: *whatever* you ask . . . if you believe . . . you *will* receive.

Then in Matthew 18:20,[2] Christ explains how your prayers are enhanced when you pray *with* someone. He said, "Where two or three gather together as my followers, I am there among them."

Those two scriptures comprise the foundation of this study group about Partnered Prayer. By that we mean married or nonmarried couples, two family members, or two friends who agree to take The 40 Day Prayer Challenge, praying together for a minimum of five minutes a day, for forty days.

Based on beta studies, authors SQuire Rushnell and Louise DuArt contend that if you pray *together,* faithfully, every day, you will join thousands of couples and partners who testify that "praying together is truly a life changing experience." In short . . . you'll be astonished!

OVERVIEW OF THIS EIGHT-WEEK STUDY GROUP

This first session is a warm-up to get you excited about the prospects of Partnered Prayer. But we also want to let you know that this is not *just* about you.

Inasmuch as you will be participating in the first empirical study ever done on what happens when two people pray together daily, the results that you and your partner experience in the next eight weeks will greatly contribute to how the world understands prayer.

The Pray Together, Stay Together organization, in association with Baylor University's Institute for Studies of Religion, is coordinating the execution of the study with thousands of churches and small groups.

In the next session, you'll begin The 40 Day Prayer Challenge by taking a ten-minute survey on your smartphone, tablet, or computer. Then, at the end of our Prayer Challenge, you'll take the wrap-up survey. At the final session, number eight, you will receive the results of your experience—available through a digital report card—showing how you and your partner were affected by the experiment. On that note, let us remind you no one other than you and the social scientists at Baylor University will see your data.

EXTRAORDINARY—YET RARE—RESEARCH

How valuable is praying with a partner regularly? Research on this question is limited, and the only data there is relates to married couples. Yet the research results from *this* experiment—which includes couples, two family members, or two friends who pray together—will add valuable insight to the question.

Dr. Tom Ellis, chairman of the Council on the Family for the Southern Baptist Convention, says, "Born-again Christian couples who marry in the church . . . after receiving premarital counseling . . . who attend church regularly and *pray daily together* . . . have a divorce rate that is approximately one divorce out of nearly 39,000!"[3]

In the introduction to this book, authors SQuire and Louise cite Baylor University research included in an earlier book of theirs, *Couples Who Pray*. Baylor was able to uncover and evaluate data from a Gallup Poll in which respondents went from "praying together sometimes" to "praying together frequently." Keeping in mind most people *never* pray together, the data from that narrowly defined survey still produced surprising outcomes. For one, social scientists discovered that for those who "prayed together frequently," the fear of divorce dropped to zero!

Group Leader Note: Decide whether the information under each discussion is applicable to the makeup of your group. Typically devote ten to fifteen minutes discussing some or all of these questions.

DISCUSSION #1. WHAT HAPPENS WHEN MARRIED COUPLES PRAY TOGETHER

Do you think there is a parallel between these two Gallup findings? When married people pray together more often:
    a. happiness rises by 18 percent, and;
    b. agreement on raising the kids goes up by 11 percent.

- People who prayed together frequently were 22 percent better at compromise. Can you remember a time when you prayed with someone about an issue and God guided you into compromise and there was a win-win outcome?
- The study showed that among those praying frequently, conversation between partners improved 11 percent. Let's discuss why you think frequent prayer would result in improved conversation between partners.
- For married people who prayed together frequently, lovemaking soared by 20 percent and marital stability became 16 percent greater. Do these two findings seem compatible to you?

DISCUSSION #2. SPEAK IT, BELIEVE IT, EXPECT IT!

A foundation of this book and study group is this scripture: "Whatever you ask in prayer, if you believe, you will receive."[4]

The authors note that God did everything by speaking it. He spoke: "Let there be light," and there was light.[5] In Genesis, God spoke, "Let Us make mankind"[6] and there were men and women. God did all of His work in the first seven days of creation by using the power of the *spoken* word.

Jesus followed in God's footsteps. Everything He did— every miracle He performed—was *spoken*. When Jesus spoke, the seas calmed.

Jesus gave that power of the spoken word to us. In Mark 11:23, He said, "If anyone says to this mountain, 'Go, throw yourself into the sea,' and does not doubt in their heart, but believes that what they say will happen, it will be done for them." Jesus asks us to *speak* to the mountains in your life— mountains of worry, debt, or shame—and He says we have the power to "speak them away."

- In Proverbs 18:21, it says, "Death and life are in the power of the tongue." If everything God commanded was by *speaking it* . . . if the miracles of Jesus were fulfilled when He *spoke* them . . . can you comprehend the power *you* have with the spoken word?

In addition to *speaking* your prayers, a critical step in getting them answered is *believing* God is who He says He is and that He can do what He says He can. In other words, if you doubt God, you are self-canceling your prayer.

- Do you find yourself struggling with an issue of doubt? Do you feel doubt "self-cancels" your prayers?

The third key to having prayers answered—in addition to *speaking* them and *believing* in God—is to *expect* an outcome. In Matthew 21:22, Jesus said, "Whatever you ask in prayer, if you *believe*, you will *receive*." He reiterates that promise in Mark 11:24, "whatever you ask for in prayer, *believe* that you *have received it*, and it will be yours."[7]

- Do you *expect* you *have already received* the answer to your prayers when you *speak* them?

Authors SQuire and Louise cite spoken words in history that have moved us. For example, John F. Kennedy's challenge "Ask not what your country can do for you . . ." and Martin Luther King Jr.'s "I have a dream . . ." were powerful words that when *spoken* seemed to take on a life of their own.

- Do you agree that there is an "invisible power to words"?
- Have you found yourself *speaking* about how bad things are? In Proverbs 12:14, the scriptures say, "A man will be satisfied with good by the fruit of his mouth." If you *speak* of bad things, not good, are you going against God's Word?

DISCUSSION #3. GODWINKS: ANOTHER WORD FOR ANSWERED PRAYER

Sir William Temple was a highly respected theological leader in Great Britain in the mid-1600s. He once said: "When I pray, coincidences happen, and when I don't, they don't."

According to SQuire Rushnell, author of the Godwinks books, Sir William's quote seems to lay the groundwork for his Godwinks thesis. He says the first meaning of *godwink* is an experience some would call "coincidence," but the odds are so extraordinary it could only have come from divine origin. And the second meaning of *godwink* is "answered prayer."

- Have you ever had "godwinks"—so-called coincidences—that you are certain came from God?
- Who has a story of a godwink that supports the author's thesis of godwinks being "answered prayers"?
- SQuire contends that our awareness of godwinks seems to increase at times of sorrow, especially after losing a loved one. Do you think that's true?
- Do you think there is merit to the author's claim that once you acknowledge your godwinks, you are more likely to see them more frequently?

ASSIGNMENT FOR NEXT SESSION

For the next session, read the introduction and chapters 1 and 2. This is the most homework you will have in the eight weeks.

- Be sure to bring your smartphone, tablet, or computer to next week's session. The first order of business will be to take the first survey in The 40 Day Prayer Challenge. It will take ten minutes or less; a second survey will be completed in the final session.
- Be thinking about who can be your "accountability partners." Next week each partnership should select another partnership to help keep you accountable.

SESSION #2

HOW PARTNERED PRAYER WORKS AND HOW TO PRAY
(Based on chapters 1 and 2)

GROUP LEADER

The 40 Day Prayer Challenge begins!

We are participating in the first empirical study ever done on what happens when two people pray together consistently for forty days. What is learned from experiences, and groups like this, will be evaluated by Baylor University's Institute for Studies of Religion. That data may change the way the world feels about prayer, and "Partnered Prayer" in particular.

It is critical to take a few moments to take the survey . . . on the first and fortieth days of the experiment journey together.

To take the survey, go to PrayStay.org. It should take no more than ten minutes to answer all questions.

These two points are important:

1. In order to participate in the survey, **each person must have their own email address.**
2. When you initially sign up on your smartphone, tablet, or computer, you and your partner must both sign up on the same device. You each will receive a unique login and pass-

word. Once you have signed up and the system knows your name, password, and the church or organization you are associated with, you can then sign in on separate devices to take the survey, or you may each take the survey on the same device one after the other.

The data for The 40 Day Prayer Challenge is totally confidential; other than you and your partner, the data is seen by no one except social scientists at Baylor University.

In forty days, when you complete your 40 Day Prayer Challenge, each set of partners will be able to download a report card—bar graphs of your achievements—demonstrating the power of prayer in your lives.

This is a good time to think about connecting with another pair of partners in this group who can be your accountability partners. While not imperative, it's advisable to identify others you can speak and meet with more frequently than just when this group meets, in order to share your progress, to discuss questions or issues, and to provide support for each other generally. Please keep in mind, your accountability partners should feel safe that you will be their confidants and not share secrets that would violate their trust.

DISCUSSION #1. JEFF WINTER'S PASTOR'S CONFESSION

Prayer is a key to a vibrant marriage. But for Jeff and Judy, their prayer life was hit-or-miss. Jeff is a pastor, and while he always prayed with his congregation and said grace with Judy, the concept of actually praying together was a penny that had never dropped. After the two of them took The 40 Day Prayer Challenge, they began a vibrant prayer life that has never stopped. They consider it a wonderful gift to share with other couples.

- Has your prayer life been hit-or-miss?
- Do you pray together only when there is a crisis?
- Do you have pride issues you need to lay aside?
- Do you think praying together will encourage meaningful and deeper conversation?

DISCUSSION #2. TIM AND KATHY KELLER

Tim Keller, pastor of the Redeemer Presbyterian Church in New York City, was brought to a life-changing insight by his wife, Kathy, in the days after the terrorist attacks on the World Trade Center on 9/11. Her feelings of depression, exacerbated by a long struggle with Crohn's disease, prompted Kathy to ask Tim to pray with her every night. "*Every* night?" he responded. She continued with simple logic: "Imagine you were . . . told that you would die unless you took a particular pill every night. Would you not get around to it? No—it would be so crucial, you wouldn't forget, you would never miss a dose."

- How does Kathy Keller's question to her husband resonate with you? Does it help put things in perspective about the importance of daily prayer?

- For Tim Keller, his wife's question was the moment "the penny dropped." He admitted anything that was "a non-negotiable necessity" was something they could do. Can you identify with the pastor's reasoning?
- As someone with a busy schedule yourself, can you understand how even a pastor can get caught up with time-demanding things and easily overlook the importance of Partnered Prayer?
- Share a story about how you think praying consistently with your partner will benefit different areas of your life.

DISCUSSION #3. DR. CHAUNCEY CRANDALL

When the Holy Spirit told Dr. Chauncey Crandall, the noted cardiologist, to turn around and pray for a dead man, he could have thought it a preposterous idea and ignored the Voice. Thankfully, he was obedient, he prayed, and the dead man came back to life.

- How has the Holy Spirit manifested in your life?
- Were there times when you ignored that "still, small voice" because your rational mind took over?
- Have you ever gotten the sense that God was asking you to do something or say something that went against your rational thinking?
- Have you ever felt that God was speaking directly to your situation as you were reading a particular passage of scripture?

DISCUSSION #4. AL AND CEIL KASHA'S STORY: WORDS PLANTED IN CHILDHOOD

Composer Al Kasha had received many accolades and financial successes—an Academy Award for "The Morning After" and great reviews for his Broadway show *Seven Brides for Seven Brothers*. Yet despite all that, his father's hurtful words from childhood created a self-imposed prison. The only way those chains could be broken was by the power of prayer and the Word of God.

In Proverbs 18:21, it says: "The tongue has the power of life and death, and those who love it will eat its fruit."

- Have you noticed it's easier to remember the hurtful words said to you than the good ones?
- Do words that were spoken to you as a child haunt you to this day?
- Do you find the memory of those words affecting decisions you make today? In what way?
- Do you say negative things to yourself like "no one cares about me" or "I'll never get out of debt"?

SUMMARY

Negative thoughts and words will block God's blessings. You need to push those preconceived ideas out of your mind and replace them with what your Heavenly Father says about you.

This week make a conscious decision to speak according to the power and authority of God's word. Every time you catch yourself saying something opposite of what His word says, like "no one cares about me," write it down. Then write down beside it a scripture to replace the negative thought with God's truth. An example of that is John 15:9, where Jesus says, "As the Father has loved me, so have I loved you. Now remain in my love."

ASSIGNMENT FOR NEXT SESSION

Read chapter 3, "Partnered Prayer," selecting the section(s) appropriate to your group. Or you can also read all three sections of chapter 3: Couples, Families, and Friends.

SESSION #3

PARTNERED PRAYER
(Based on chapter 3)

GROUP LEADER

Determine the appropriate subgroup below that fits your needs:
- A: Couples
- B: Families
- C: Friends

Group Leader Note: It will be up to you to determine how many discussion points from the three subsections are taken up by your group; for example, couples, in section A, may wish to select discussion points from section B pertaining to family members praying together.

You may also choose to use some or all of the following on-line links to testimonials to use during this session with couples.

Video Links

1. Tiffany and Matt (55 seconds, http://youtu.be/jUyGh FG-rCQ): A young couple learn that praying together helps pregnancy.

2. Sandy and Paul (50 seconds, http://youtu.be/zlfOD1 ulO8): After Paul's vulnerability, prayer helps Sandy see his heart.

3. Kandice and Mike (1:00 minute, http://youtu.be/R9ip EBGSaW8): Prayer becomes amazingly joyful after an awkward start.

4. Various couples (45 seconds, https://youtu.be/zYds7iwSro): A quick summary with four couples on praying together.

PARTNERED PRAYER STORIES

You have now had the opportunity to experience Partnered Prayer for one week.

Let's take a few minutes to share your surprises, challenges, and successes.

The authors wish to note that your stories of Partnered Prayer may help others by posting them at PrayStay.org.

A: COUPLES

(Based on chapter 3, section A)

GROUP LEADER

Authors SQuire Rushnell and Louise DuArt have written that "starting to pray together may seem like a vast, scary, unfamiliar bridge to cross. Yet, by taking that first step—holding your partner's hand and just listening—it becomes merely a footbridge. And you can't imagine the joy that awaits you on the other side."

DISCUSSION #1. ERICK AND LESLIE: RELUCTANCE TO PRAY TOGETHER

Erick was highly reluctant to pray with Leslie, but over time he became more and more invested. You'll recall he started out sitting at the kitchen table just listening to Leslie pray, but he eventually ending up on the couch next to her, actively participating.

- What do you think are the root causes for one partner to be less willing to pray together than the other?
- Do you find yourself guarding against being too vulnerable in front of your partner?
- Do you believe God can mend your relationship and make it better than ever?
- What adjustments can you make in your schedules to spend time in prayer with your Creator?

DISCUSSION #2. ROSS AND LEAH

Every hurtful comment Ross and Leah hurled at each other created another brick in a wall that rose higher and higher until it became a total barrier to love and joy between them. Their options had run out, and in desperation they made one

210   SQuire Rushnell and Louise DuArt

last-ditch effort to do what SQuire and Louise suggested—
pray together.

God honored their choice to be obedient and to pray together even though they didn't feel like it. God did not just
create a crack in the wall: He blew it up! Prayer was the dyna-
mite that broke through and opened their hearts to receive the
blessings God wanted them to experience.

- Like Ross and Leah, do you think praying together can
give your relationship a fresh start?
- Why do you suppose humbling yourself before God,
and your partner, opens the way to a renewed relationship?
- Do you feel you have become complacent and taken
your spouse for granted?
- What things can you do to relight the fire that was once
there?

Discussion #3. Pam and Jay: Looking Like the "Perfect" Couple

On the outside, Pam and Jay had all the appearances of a
perfect marriage. But it was a façade. Behind the curtain, as
Pam says, "We mentioned divorce, but we were too lazy. It
was easier not to talk at all; when we did, it was usually disrespectful."

- When you see a "perfect couple" like Pam and Jay, do
you find yourself assuming their lives are more together
than yours?

- Do you believe some people continue to stay together, even though the joy is gone, due to the fear of hurting their children or losing their security?
- When you go through difficult times, does it draw you closer to your partner, or do you find it pulls you apart?
- Do you feel that humbling yourselves before each other and God will draw you closer and bring back the joy you once had or increase the joy you already have?

DISCUSSION #4. KESLEIGH AND CHAD: LISTENING TO EACH OTHER

Kesleigh writes: "It's just amazing to be held by my husband, listening to him verbally thank God for the gift he was given. What could be better than *hearing* my husband acknowledge the difficult job of mothering four kids, keeping up with a house, and trying to work outside the home?"

- The Baylor/Gallup study indicated an 11 percent improvement in conversation between partners who pray together frequently. Do you think prayer helps us to become better *listeners*?
- How do you think prayer will enhance your respect for each other?
- The best way you can honor your partner is to pray for each other. What are some words you can say that will honor him or her?
- Do you feel safe to talk candidly about your weaknesses and struggles with God in the presence of your spouse? If not, what is holding you back?

ASSIGNMENT FOR NEXT SESSION

Read chapter 4, "Churches That Pray Together."

B: FAMILIES

(Based on chapter 3, section B)

GROUP LEADER

Authors SQuire Rushnell and Louise DuArt write, "We know the outcome prayer has when couples pray together; the results are phenomenal . . . yet the concept of Partnered Prayer works the same for a mother and daughter, a sister and her brother, or any combination of family members. Arguments are likely to diminish, if not go away altogether; sharing, thoughtfulness, and respect will increase; and happiness is likely to rise."

DISCUSSION #1. LEARNING TO PRAY AS A CHILD

Many people—if not most—were never taught to pray as children, other than prayer by rote, such as "Now I lay me down to sleep." It is, therefore, little surprise so many adults simply do not know how to pray.

- Were you taught how to pray as a child?
- If you learned the "Now I lay me down to sleep" prayer, did it scare you?

- Do you agree that the family structure is under attack and it's important to fight the battle together in prayer?
- Do you ask your children to thank God for the blessings He has given to them?
- How do you approach children so they will open up about matters worrying them?

DISCUSSION #2. DOES GOD HEAR AND REMEMBER THE PRAYERS OF CHILDREN?

Louise DuArt and Tim Conway, comedians who performed together, discovered they had similar experiences at about the age of twelve; they both had prayed for specific things, and both of their prayers were answered.

- What did Louise DuArt and Tim Conway have in common?
- Do you feel many of your hopes and dreams as a child have come and gone?
- What hopes and dreams did you pray for as a child? Did they come true?
- Do you believe it is too late to accomplish every desire God placed in your heart?

DISCUSSION #3. JIM AND KAREN COVELL'S FAMILY PRAYERS

The founders of the Hollywood Prayer Network turned their daily family prayer time with their two boys into a creative and even fun experience.

- What intrigues you the most about the Covell family's prayer policy?
- Do you have games you can play with your kids to stimulate prayer?
- Do you believe that instilling biblical truths in your children at an early age will provide spiritual direction for the rest of their lives?
- How do you set an example for your kids to teach them biblical principles such as forgiveness?

DISCUSSION #4. MARIAN CHADWICK'S STORY

When an armed robber walked into Marian Chadwick's store, she faced him down with her own weapon—the Word of God.

- What is the primary message in Marian's story?
- Do you think Marian's childhood biblical teachings have held her in good stead?
- Do you believe in Marian's strategy—that the best way to stop an attack is to counterattack with the word of God?
- What is the best way to memorize scripture so that when the Enemy attacks, you can instantly quote God's prom-

ises? Do you put scriptures on the refrigerator, or on sticky notes, postcards, etc.?

ASSIGNMENT FOR NEXT SESSION

Read chapter 4, "Churches That Pray Together."

C: FRIENDS

(Based on chapter 3, section C)

GROUP LEADER

God has amazing arithmetic. He teaches us that when we pray alone, it is effective, but when two or more are united in prayer, the power increases tremendously and so do the outcomes. Listen to this promise:

> *One of you shall chase a thousand,*
> *but two of you shall chase ten thousand.*
> —DEUTERONOMY 32:30, NIV

SQuire and Louise write, "We all sail into life's storms. But navigating the rough seas all by yourself is more difficult. With a prayer partner to help you bail out depression and discouragement, and raise your sails of faith, you'll be blessed by extra measures of God's wind at your back to overcome the most painful of times."

DISCUSSION #1. DEE AND GLORIA

Two friends, Dee and Gloria, have walked side by side in their prayer journey. There have been bleak days where one held up the other, and there have been joyful days when they rejoiced in victory. Through it all, the two friends learned to praise God for their challenges as well as their blessings, one of which is their bond of friendship.

- When Dee and Gloria were going through their challenging life experiences, they had a choice. They could choose fear or faith. What is your observation about that?
- Have you ever had a desperate need and your prayer partner girded you up and helped you choose faith over fear? Would you share your story?
- When Dee had cancer, she realized that through praying with Gloria, they could take a terrible experience and praise God for it. Have you ever done that?
- Have you had a heart-wrenching experience that God has used to touch someone else's life?

SUMMARY

In Dee and Gloria's prayer partnership, the investment they made in each other's lives produced great rewards. They felt it was important to keep a prayer journal. When they looked back at what they had written at a later time, they were encouraged; it built their faith to see clearly how God had answered specific prayers.

DISCUSSION #2. THE BLESSINGS OF A PRAYER PARTNERSHIP

Praying with a friend is a blessing; six ways are described in this book.

- What do you think about the premise that praying together will help remove feelings of aloneness?
- Being accountable to one another is a benefit of Partnered Prayer—do you agree?
- The authors contend praying with a friend allows you both to become stronger in the Lord. What's your view?
- Partnered Prayer relies on this scripture to help us to become a stronger force against the enemy: "Two are better than one. . . for if they fall, one will lift up his fellow. But woe to him who is alone when he falls and has not another to lift him up" (Ecclesiastes 4:9–10, NIV). Discuss.

DISCUSSION #3. THE PRINCIPLES OF FAITH

Faith is something you can't see but through it, you can expect the existence of things you have prayed for. The King James Bible spells it out this way:

Faith is the substance of things hoped for,
the evidence of things not seen.

In more contemporary language, another Bible version, The Word, says:

> *Faith assures us of things we expect,*
> *and convinces us of the existence*
> *of things we cannot see.*
> —HEBREWS 1:11, KJV

- In Corinthians 5:7, we are told we should "live by faith, not by sight." Explain.
- We are asked in Ephesians 6:16 to "Take up the shield of faith with which you can extinguish all the flaming arrows of the evil one." What does that mean?
- Have you ever felt you have been controlled by things you see, such as a bad medical report, poor finances, or family complications, and it was difficult for you to have faith?
- How has prayer and God's word helped you to move away from worry and into the area of faith and not sight?

DISCUSSION #4. TEN WAYS TO STRENGTHEN YOUR FAITH

The authors have laid out ten ways we can strengthen our faith. They noted the following scripture passage sums up ways to strengthen faith:

> *Confess your sins to one another and pray for one another,*
> *that you may be healed. The prayer of a righteous person*
> *has great power.*
> —JAMES 5:16, ESV

- The contention that "a prayer partner builds your faith" asserts that your engagement in daily prayer with another person will help you to support and encourage one another. Do you agree? And can you elaborate on that?
- "Faith is like a muscle" and "learning to wait on the Lord" are compatible tips on building your faith. In the first, you are keeping fit by *exercising* prayer; in the other, you are trusting God by learning to *stand*. How do you see these two points working within your prayer partnership?
- In Romans 8:28 (NLT) we are told that "God causes everything to work together for the good of those who love God and are called according to His purpose for them." How can your trials help build your faith?
- "Giving testimony enhances faith," according to authors SQuire and Louise. Has your testimony about how God intervened in your life helped build the faith of others?

Assignment for Next Session

Read chapter 4, "Churches That Pray Together."

SESSION #4

CHURCHES THAT PRAY TOGETHER
(Based on chapter 4)

GROUP LEADER

Authors SQuire Rushnell and Louise DuArt write, "We so admire church families that rally around their own. When someone's home burns to the ground, it's the churches that are the first to pitch in. When a hurricane like Katrina wipes out great sections of a state, it's the churches that are the first on the scene, feeding and clothing the displaced."

In this session we focus on the amazing stories of four church communities that pulled together at a time of crisis to rally around those in need.

But first . . .

PARTNERED PRAYER STORIES

You have now experienced Partnered Prayer for two weeks. What's the most amazing thing that has happened since you have been praying together?

And, as a reminder, SQuire and Louise invite you to share your stories of challenges and victories at PrayStay.org.

DISCUSSION #1. JIM CYMBALA'S STORY

Jim Cymbala's story about the Brooklyn Tabernacle Church exemplifies how absolutely necessary it is for a congregation to be dependent on prayer to carry out God's work.

- Jim Cymbala had no experience, no theological degree, yet the Lord was selecting him to lead a rundown church in Brooklyn. Can you think of other highly unlikely candidates God has employed in His causes?
- How critical was the prayer of a unified congregation to the survival of the church?
- Jim Cymbala stopped his sermon, broke into tears, and confessed, "If God doesn't help us, I don't know what we'll do." Why do you suppose God needs us to reach the breaking point in order for Him to step in?
- Pastor Jim sensed an inner voice saying, "If you and your wife will lead my people to pray and to call upon my name, you will never lack; I will supply what's needed . . . and you will never have a building large enough to contain the crowds." Can you think of a comparable experience where God assured someone He was going to bless them mightily?

DISCUSSION #2. PETER VINCENT'S EXPERIENCE

When Peter Vincent was given little hope, the Beacon of Hope Church on the island of Martha's Vineyard went on high alert and prayed around the clock. Peter and his family believe it was the power of prayer that saved his life.

- Charles Spurgeon, one of Britain's great preachers in the 1800s, believed in fervent prayer. He said, "Prayer pulls the rope below, and the great bell rings above in the ears of God. Some scarcely stir the bell, for they pray so languidly; others give but an occasional pluck at the rope; but he who wins with heaven is the man who grasps the rope boldly and pulls continuously, with all his might." [8] How have you and your church prayed with "all your might" for God to release His healing power?

- When Missy Vincent was told that her husband had died and was revived twice, she prayed, "Father God, You are in control—please keep my husband alive." She then put out the urgent word to her church to increase their prayers. Do you believe abundant and fervent prayers—pulling on the rope to the bells in heaven—changed the balance, resulting in Peter Vincent's survival?

- If prayer puts God to work on earth, does the lack of prayer rule out, or diminish, God's intervention on someone's healing?

- When Peter "coded," he found himself in a peaceful place with bright whiteness; he says he now has "no fear of death." Do you believe he experienced heaven?

DISCUSSION #3. JOHN SMITH'S AMAZING MIRACLE

Fourteen-year-old John Smith was without a pulse for nearly an hour; he had been submerged under the ice for fifteen minutes before doctors tried urgently to revive him for another forty-five minutes. As he was about to be declared dead, his mother, Joyce Smith, said, "Holy Spirit, give me back my son." The next sound was a medical technician shouting, "We've got a pulse!" Sixteen days later, John Smith walked out of the hospital with no damage to his brain, lungs, or internal organs.

- Two doctors and several first responders labeled John Smith's case a miracle. His survival could be explained by no other means, except that there was a massive beseeching of prayers from his family, his church, and thousands over social networks. Do you suppose God has a special purpose for healing John Smith?
- Have you experienced a miracle? Would you share your story?
- John was still in a coma when Joyce Smith met with doctors at the hospital. She said, "You do what you do best, and my God will do the rest." Would you say that Joyce's faith never wavered?
- Joyce quotes Proverbs 18:21: "Death and life are in the power of the tongue." She believes that *speaking* prayers and scripture, and calling upon the Holy Spirit, were essential to God answering her prayer. Do you agree?

DISCUSSION #4. TOM RENFRO'S CHURCH SUPPORT

Dr. Tom Renfro was given no hope; grapefruit-size tumors had popped up all over his body. His church formed teams to pray for him, around the clock, for more than eighty days. The congregation remained undeterred by Tom's circumstances or the medical community's dire prognosis. They were firm in their belief. They *spoke* their prayers for Tom, truly *believed* God was hearing their appeal for healing and that they could *expect* a desirable outcome.

Miraculously, the tumors began to disappear. Today, Dr. Tom Renfro is back to treating patients and sharing his testimony.

- Two weeks after his healing, Tom Renfro, a medical doctor, stood in front of his church with tears of joy. He said, "I don't have the words to express what is in my heart . . . this is a true miracle . . . this is what you have been praying for." Do you think that the congregation's faith—keeping their eyes on Jesus rather than the circumstances—made all the difference?
- How has community prayer brought people closer to one another in your church?
- How have you stood firm in faith when the doctors gave someone you love little hope of surviving?
- Authors SQuire and Louise write, "Persistence of prayer and the expectation of a successful outcome surely play critical roles . . . but part of the mystery of God is why He allows some to be healed and not others. Even the

apostle Paul, who had amazing faith, did not get healed after he asked God three times." We therefore cannot speculate that someone who *doesn't* get healed is lacking in faith. Do you know someone who was more like the apostle Paul and wasn't healed, as opposed to someone like Dr. Renfro, who was?

ASSIGNMENT FOR NEXT SESSION

Read chapter 5, "When Our Nation Prayed."

others who have struggled with similar issues. You can share your story at PrayStay.org.

DISCUSSION #1. BEN FRANKLIN'S APPEAL

The Founding Fathers had exhaustively debated the drafting of the US Constitution for five weeks and were in an impossible logjam. Eighty-one-year-old Benjamin Franklin rose to his feet and eloquently addressed his colleagues. He reminded them that during the war they had beseeched God on a daily basis. "Our prayers were heard, sirs, and they were graciously answered," he said. Shortly after Franklin's speech asking all participants to pray, the deadlock mysteriously broke and America had a Constitution.

- Alexander Hamilton said of Franklin's initiative that the system of governance for our country "never could have been . . . agreed upon by such a diversity of interests" without "the finger of God." Would you agree with Hamilton?
- Have you been in a situation that was deadlocked, and through the power of prayer, God mysteriously opened doors that were previously slammed shut?
- Does prayer guide your life, or is it your last resort when trouble strikes? Do you have an experience where prayer should have been your first line of defense, not your last?
- Have you ever felt confused and needed clarity about something when you finally came to the conclusion that God had the answer all along and all you had to do was pray?

SESSION #5

WHEN OUR NATION PRAYED
(Based on chapter 5)

GROUP LEADER

We generally think of prayer as something that is articulated between individuals and God, relating to matters of health, finance, or peace of mind. We don't often think about prayer directing a nation. Of course, the question is, why not? If God is in control of our lives, wouldn't He also be involved in matters of state?

In chapter 5, SQuire and Louise focus our attention on individuals who played key roles at the helm of America, and how prayer, at auspicious times, was critical to how things worked out.

Before that, though . . .

PARTNERED PRAYER STORIES

Let's hear some stories. You're halfway through The 40 Day Prayer Challenge—praying together for three weeks. Can we take a few moments to share some surprises and successes?

A reminder: your testimony may help untold numbers of

THE 40 DAY PRAYER CHALLENGE   229

- Let's discuss the Benjamin Franklin quote "Work as if you were to live a hundred years. Pray as if you were to die tomorrow."

DISCUSSION #2. BULLETPROOF GEORGE WASHINGTON

Our first president had gotten four bullets through his coat and two horses shot out from under him during a battle, but he emerged unscathed. He wrote to his mother and brother, "By the all-powerful dispensations of Providence I have been protected beyond all human probability or expectation." In George Washington's case, the ancient scriptures were proven right:

No weapon that is formed against you shall prosper.
—ISAIAH 54:17, AKJV

- Six years prior to the signing of the Declaration of Independence, a Native American chief recalled the aforementioned battle. The chief had assigned his warriors the task of firing their rifles at Washington. He said, "we knew not how to miss . . . but a power mightier than we shielded" him. He then prophesied, "people yet unborn will hail him as the founder of a mighty empire." Do you believe God was saving Washington for a greater purpose?
- Have you been in a crisis situation where the worst was about to happen, but through divine providence you were saved?

- In their writings, America's founders unashamedly spoke using scripture and were strong in their faith. Do you believe our country could once more benefit from those practices?
- For 150 years, until it was removed four decades ago, the heroic George Washington story was part of the teachings of American history in schools. Should that part of history be restored for our children?

DISCUSSION #3. HOW PRAYER SAVED EISENHOWER

Supported by his brother, Dwight Eisenhower refused to allow doctors to amputate his infected leg. Yet he was miraculously healed through the fervent prayers of his family, placing him on a divine path to become our thirty-fourth president.

- Eisenhower's parents encouraged independence for their boys, balanced with hard work and faith in God. Where do you see these values in short supply today?
- Eisenhower and his brother, raised in a poor family, worked to help each other through college. Tell us your observations about how kids who are disadvantaged have risen above their circumstances, giving them a unique advantage over other kids who feel entitled.
- If Eisenhower had had his leg amputated as a teenager, as the doctors had recommended, he could never have entered the military. And the military was his pathway to the presidency. Do you believe that the outcome was

God's plan, through the divine alignment of godwinks and events?

- Has God intervened in a particular situation and supernaturally changed the course of your life?

DISCUSSION #4. THE SURPRISING GOVERNMENT STATS ON SCHOOL PRAYER

Historian David Barton graphically illustrates how America has been plummeting from righteous living into an immoral society that oftentimes shuns biblical principles. He makes his case that much of it began when prayer was removed from public schools.

- Have you seen the effect that the removal of prayer has had on certain parts of our society?
- David Barton showed that the year after prayer was removed from public schools, the government's own data demonstrates that birth rates began to soar among unwed teenage girls, doubling in the next twenty years. Do you believe there is a correlation?
- Have you observed an incident that was unjust or corrupt because people turned their back on God?
- How do you explain biblical principles to your children when something they've seen or heard goes directly against what the Bible teaches?

ASSIGNMENT FOR NEXT SESSION

Read chapter 6, "The Enemy Is Real."

SESSION #6

THE ENEMY IS REAL
(Based on chapter 6)

GROUP LEADER

In this session we are talking about a part of spiritual life that gets little of our attention: the Enemy. And the Enemy is probably pleased with that. He likes to stay in the shadows of your life, slinking around like a robber casing your home.

Authors SQuire Rushnell and Louise DuArt suggest it is natural for us to put the majority of our focus on the ideal spiritual life written in Hebrews:

Let us run with perseverance the race marked out for us,
fixing our eyes on Jesus, the pioneer and perfecter of faith.[9]

Yet as we run the race every day, seeking to emulate Christ, we must never let our guard down. As prayer partners, we must watch each other's backs. We cannot become complacent, ignoring what we know about the Enemy:

Your enemy, the devil, prowls around like a roaring lion
looking for someone to devour. Resist him, standing firm
in the faith.
—I PETER 5:8; NIV

First, though, it is time to share some of your testimony.

PARTNERED PRAYER STORIES

You have now had the opportunity to experience Partnered Prayer for four weeks.

You probably have had some opposition from the Enemy, but also surprises and successes.

As always, SQuire and Louise remind you that your growing understanding about Partnered Prayer can encourage others at PrayStay.org.

DISCUSSION #1. GETTING TO KNOW THE ENEMY

Written five hundred years before Christ, the ancient Chinese strategy *The Art of War* has been studied by military leaders of nearly every nation. A central thesis of its author, Sun Tzu is this:

> *If you know the enemy and know yourself,*
> *you need not fear the result of a hundred battles.*
> *If you know yourself but not the enemy,*
> *for every victory gained you will also suffer a defeat.*
> *If you know neither the enemy nor yourself,*
> *you will succumb in every battle.*

The bottom line: to defeat an enemy, you must know his strengths and weaknesses. But you also need to know your own.

- SQuire and Louise have labeled the Enemy as the "Dis of Darkness" because he loves everything "dis"—dishonesty, distraction, discouragement—anything to cause discombobulation, distress, and disturbance. Would you agree with this characterization of the Enemy—that he's the "Dis of Darkness"? Do you have other observations about his DISruptions?
- The enemy goes for your weak spots. SQuire says the Enemy goes for his "pride"; for Louise, it's her "anxiety." What about you—have you asked God to show you where you're the most vulnerable?
- Have you ever invited someone to come into your home or life who the Enemy was using as a Trojan horse? Did he or she use temptation, division, or false teaching?
- Do you agree with the statement "Most of the power the Enemy ever has . . . is what you give him"?

DISCUSSION #2. WHAT IT MEANS: PUTTING ON THE FULL ARMOR

The ancient scriptures tells us in Ephesians to:

Put on the full armor of God,
so that you will be able to stand firm
against the schemes of the devil.[10]

- How do you interpret "put on the full armor of God"?
- If you knew then what you know now, how would you have dealt with an entrapment by the Enemy in which you found yourself?

- Ephesians also says, "our struggle is not against flesh and blood, but against . . . the powers . . . of darkness."[11] What is your take on that?
- The authors asked, "Was there a time when you were lured into the shadows by the Enemy . . . keeping secrets . . . or perhaps controlled by addictive behavior?" Scripture says, in James 4:7, "Submit yourself to God . . . then . . . resist the devil, and he will flee from you."[12] How have you been able to resist the Enemy? Did he flee?

DISCUSSION #3. WHAT IS YOUR WEAPONRY AGAINST THE ENEMY?

- We are told to pick up "the sword of the Spirit"[13]—the Bible—described as "sharper than any double-edged sword."[14] Do you agree that God's word is the greatest weapon against the enemy?
- "The Helmet of Salvation"[15] protects your head and mind, say the scriptures. Do you concur the Enemy will try to infect you with doubt and discouragement while luring you into his snare? Give examples of how he did.
- You are told to "Take up the shield of faith" to protect you from "the flaming arrows of the evil one."[16] Would you agree that this armament protects your body from venomous words, disease, or body blows?
- It says in Luke 10:19: "Behold I give unto you power to tread on serpents and scorpions, and over all the power

of the enemy: and nothing shall by any means hurt you."
He will try to trick you, seduce you, con you, or to lie to
you, but if you remain grounded in truth and faith, isn't
the Enemy really powerless?

DISCUSSION #4. THE JEZEBEL SPIRIT

Authors SQuire Rushnell and Louise DuArt write, "There
is a vile demonic spirit that the Enemy sets loose, particularly in churches, taking root in people who knowingly or
unknowingly allow it. It's identified as the Jezebel spirit, and
while it inhabits women more frequently, it also inhabits
some men." This is a genuine evil force that "aims to infiltrate a church, targeting the pastor and others in authority. The spirit is an excellent counterfeit. It will come as an
'angel of light.'"

- Would you agree with what author Jennifer LeClaire
  says in her book *The Spiritual Warrior's Guide to Defeating Jezebel*: "Satan's greatest deception is convincing the
  world he does not exist." So is it "Jezebel's greatest deception" to convince people that she or he is harmless?
- Steve Sampson, author of *Confronting Jezebel*, says that
  three of twenty ways to identify Jezebel are: they refuse
  to admit guilt; they take credit for everything; and volunteer for anything in order to establish control. Have
  you encountered someone like that?
- Sampson also identifies a Jezebel as someone who lies,
  criticizes everyone, sequesters information, then, sharing

tidbits of information with you, leverages it for power. Is that anyone you know?

- Robert Morris, pastor of Gateway Church in Dallas, says there was a season when a Jezebel spirit was functioning in his church. He is quoted as saying, "Jezebel will not depart easily. But with prayer and fasting, you can gain the strength for the long haul." Does Pastor Morris's prescription to begin the process of removing the Jezebel spirit make sense to you?

ASSIGNMENT FOR NEXT SESSION

Read chapter 7, "Hearing the Voice of God."

SESSION #7

HEARING THE VOICE OF GOD
(Based on chapter 7)

GROUP LEADER

Does God really speak to some people in an audible voice and to others through an inner still, small voice? Those questions usually prompt another from someone, such as "Why doesn't He speak to me?" In this chapter, SQuire and Louise presented several extraordinary stories. They varied from Polly, who heard "a man's voice [that] spoke firmly into her left ear," to Hubie Synn, the modern-day prophet who hears an inner instruction to go up to a complete stranger and give them "a word from the Lord." He has no idea what that "word" is . . . either before or after he gives it. Then SQuire and Louise shared numerous stories of mothers who received an internal message to check on their child right away. In each case the child was in danger. So in this session we are talking about "Hearing the Voice of God."

First, though, we need to hear what has happened in your next-to-last week of The 40 Day Prayer Challenge.

PARTNERED PRAYER STORIES

You have now had the opportunity to experience Partnered Prayer for five weeks. Who has a story about a surprising success or breakthrough?

DISCUSSION #1. POLLY'S URGENT VOICE COMMAND

The male "voice" from the church pew behind Polly said, "If you want to see your son alive again, you need to ask for prayer now!" Discovering no one was seated behind her, Polly stood, interrupting the pastor's sermon. She asked for urgent prayer for her son, a marine in Iraq. She was relieved to learn that several people immediately started to pray. It was two weeks later that her son called home. In the course of the conversation, he said that fourteen days earlier a sniper's bullet had whizzed past the spot he had just been occupying. He had turned a second earlier, thinking he'd heard someone behind him. No one was there. Polly's son had no idea that she and her church were praying for his safety at that moment.

- If you had been Polly and thought you'd heard a voice, would you have stood and interrupted the pastor's sermon?
- Polly heard an audible voice in her left ear sounding like it was coming from behind her. Have you ever heard an out-loud "voice" like that?
- Was Polly's prayer request strengthened by the prayers of others? If so, do you believe this was God's way of

allowing her to bridge the natural and the supernatural worlds?

• Polly said, "I dare not think what if I had not been obedient to God . . . not listened." Do you believe God was rewarding Polly's obedience?

DISCUSSION #2. HOW HUBIE HEARS GOD'S VOICE

Hubie Synn is a shy accountant to whom God seems to speak. Through a strong inner voice, Hubie is directed to "give a word from the Lord" to complete strangers. One such person was Jonathan Cahn, who was sitting in a busy airport praying for God to provide him with a sign as to what he should do with the manuscript God had nudged him to write, *The Harbinger*. Jonathan's problem: he didn't know any publishers. When Hubie, a stranger, stood before him and said, "God wants you to know that your book is going to reach many people," Jonathan was astonished. Even more so when Hubie said he knew one publisher. Hubie put the two parties together, and a year or so later, *The Harbinger* was starting its 120-week run on the *New York Times* bestsellers list.

• Can you imagine yourself as a shy person going up to a complete stranger in a busy airport and telling them that you have a "word from God," even though you have no idea what words are going to come out of your mouth, nor will you be able to remember what you said?

• Hubie Synn says, "I talk to God all the time." This leads to God's talking to him. Moreover, he thinks each of us has the capacity to be a prophet . . . we just need to get closer and closer to God. How do you feel about that?

- A characteristic of Hubie's inner nudging is that if he delays approaching a stranger, a feeling of nausea comes over him. Once he felt an inner urge to speak to a new client, a New York Giants football player. Hubie worried he might lose the new client if he approached him. Feelings of sickness rose in his stomach, but Hubie followed God's will. In the end, the player, David Tyrell, had the experience Hubie had prophesied; he gained a national platform to talk about the gospel due to a catch called "the greatest play in Super Bowl history." Can you imagine being obedient to God to the degree that you worried you might lose a business client?

- Hubie Synn contends that his work as a prophet is a matter of trust: trusting that when he steps out in faith, God will always be there to prevent him from falling on his face, and that God's words, not Hubie's, will emerge from his lips. Can you see yourself having that much trust in God?

DISCUSSION #3. THE INTUITIVE VOICE A MOTHER HEARS

In the book, several letters from mothers are shared. The common denominator: each mother received a powerful inner "Voice" or urge to act, usually to save a child!

- As a mother, have you ever had an overwhelming inner urge to check on your child?

- One mother, obeying the internal "Check on her *now*" command, discovered her child being strangled by an unraveled crib bumper guard. Can you identify with the mother's question "What if I had not heeded that voice?"
- Can you imagine the surprise of the mother who heard a voice telling her not to hold her little boy during X-rays—that she was pregnant—only to later discover that she indeed *was*?
- How many have said "There but for the grace of God go I" upon reading the story of Alisha, the mother who did *not* listen to the voice and tragically learned later that her teenage boy had taken his own life?

DISCUSSION #4. WAYS TO KNOW THAT IT'S GOD SPEAKING TO YOU

SQuire and Louise have culled the thoughts of prophets and others who have heard the voice on various occasions to devise a list: "Five Ways to Know It's God Speaking."

- Romans says, "Faith comes from hearing the message, and the message is heard through the word about Christ." [17] Do you believe that "faith is always present" as evidence of God, as stated in the Bible?
- Does it make sense to you that "God's message always agrees with scripture"—that God would never tell you to do something that does not align with His Word?
- Do these two points sound reasonable: "God usually confirms His message with a sign" and often it comes to you "through prayer"?

- Do you believe this statement is true or false: "The inner nudgings grow stronger with time"?

ASSIGNMENT FOR NEXT SESSION

Read chapter 8, "Growing in Your Prayer Together."

This is your final week of The 40 Day Prayer Challenge. Next week, be sure to have your smartphone, tablet, or computer so that you and your partner can again take the Baylor University survey. Again, you will take it individually, then you and your partner will receive a personal report card of your progress.

SESSION #8

GROWING IN YOUR PRAYER TOGETHER
(Based on chapter 8)

GROUP LEADER

This is the session of The 40 Day Prayer Challenge that is the most joyful! You've now completed the first phase of a magnificent journey—discovering something you never knew existed and could never have imagined would be so fulfilling! You have become a champion at Partnered Prayer!

In a few minutes, we want to hear your victorious Partnered Prayer stories. But first, let's find out how well you've done from day one until now. Let's take the last part of the Baylor University study.

Everyone signed in with a separate email address. If you each have a device—a smartphone, tablet, or computer—go now to PrayStay.org and log in.

If you are both using the same device, you'll need to take the survey one at a time. Again, the only way to participate in the survey is with a digital device. Let's get started.

Group Leader Note: You may wish to give your gathering five to ten minutes to complete the survey. As slower participants are wrapping up, review the following summary of objectives for those who now have your attention. Your group may also wish to take extra time now to look at their bar graphs showing how well they did versus others in the group.

While some of you finish up, let me take a few moments to reiterate the objectives of The 40 Day Prayer Challenge and why this experience was not only important to you and your partner and those who benefited from any of your altered behavior, such as your families and workplace colleagues. You have also contributed significantly to a very important endeavor.

As was outlined at the beginning, the Pray Together, Stay Together organization, in association with Baylor University's prestigious Institute for Studies of Religion, is working with churches across our nation to encourage Partnered Prayer.

The study you are finishing up right now is a critical piece of that overall objective. This is the first empirical study ever done on what happens when two people commit to praying together, every day, for an extended period.

If your weekly testimonies to each other are any measure, the outcome from this first-ever study may change how people—and churches—view their relationships with God. As partners, your lives will have changed for the better. As churches, prayer is on its way to having a higher priority.

But if this experience results in hundreds of thousands or millions of people developing habits of Partnered Prayer, then communities and nations will be the benefactors.

If what you've been participating in becomes a movement, it can literally save the world!

For your participation over the past seven weeks, we want to thank you.

Partnered Prayer Stories (allow extra time)

Today we are allowing extra time for this segment because this may be the most important question that has been asked to date: What is the *best thing* about your experience of praying together with your partner? Tell us your stories of victory!

Discussion #1. Why Stop Praying Together?

The overall direction of this discussion is "Why would you stop?" If it has been an amazing journey for you, if your relationships have improved, and your life is better, why quit?

- So, if Partnered Prayer has been a good thing, why not keep it going as part of your newly established daily routine?
- What would you say about Partnered Prayer to two people who were about to start The 40 Day Prayer Challenge?
- Was there one story or one piece of data that particularly changed your thinking about what to expect with Partnered Prayer?

DISCUSSION #2. THE MOST MEMORABLE PRAYER STORIES

You have heard many remarkable stories in this book. Let's take a few moments to discuss which ones were the most memorable for you.

- In chapter 1, we read about the simple appeal to Pastor Tim Keller from his wife, Kathy, comparing the importance of praying together daily with a medication that had been prescribed to save your life. In the same chapter was cardiologist Chauncey Crandall's story of hearing the command of the Holy Spirit to pray for a dead man. Let's discuss the impact these stories had on you.
- In the chapter that called you to "partner up and pray," we have these memorable stories:

    Under "Couples," you heard Leslie's story about Erick's evolution from the kitchen table to sitting next to her, holding her hand on the couch. Pam described how she and Jay were considered the "perfect couple," but they were living a lie—until they began to pray daily. How have they opened up your spiritual mind?

    Under "Families," how did Tim Conway's childhood discovery about the power of prayer affect you compared to the Covell family's highly creative prayers with their children?

    Under "Friends," would we agree that Dee's and Gloria's journals were indeed memorable?
- In chapter 4, "Churches That Pray Together," the amazing stories ranged from Jim Cymbala's broken pew ush-

ering in a new era for Brooklyn Tabernacle Church to what happened when a church community organized a prayer vigil for fourteen-year-old John Smith to beseech God to bring him back to life an hour after drowning. Which of those stories stirred your thinking the most?

• In our nation's history, which story resonated with you more: Benjamin Franklin calling for prayer to break a deadlock at the Constitutional Convention, or how George Washington emerged from a battle with four bullet holes in his coat and no wounds?

• Will you find yourself thinking about Polly standing up in church asking for prayer for her soldier son, or Alisha, the mother who remains tormented because she didn't respond to the "Voice" telling her to go home?

• SQuire Rushnell said that one of the best-ever god-wink stories was when Toni prayed for her husband, David, to be healed; but she also *spoke* to God about a sign . . . for it to snow on Christmas Day, for the first time ever, in their southern border community. Would you agree that's an amazing godwink or answered prayer?

GROUP LEADER

Thanks, everyone, for coming. Here's our prayer: for you to keep on praying together. After all . . . if it has done so much to improve your lives, why stop now? In fact, why not tell everyone about The 40 Day Prayer Challenge . . . the joys can be theirs, too!

APPENDIX: PRAYER PROMISES

MATTHEW 21:22
*If you **believe**, you will receive whatever
you **ask** for in **prayer**.*

ROMANS 12:12
*Rejoice in hope, be patient in tribulation,
be constant in **prayer**.*

PHILIPPIANS 4:6
*Do not be anxious about anything,
but in every situation, by **prayer** and petition,
with thanksgiving, present your requests to God.*

JAMES 5:16
*The earnest **prayer** of a righteous person
has great power and produces wonderful results.*

MARK 11:24
*Therefore I tell you, whatever you **ask** for in **prayer**,
believe that you have received it, and it will be yours.*

JAMES 5:16
*Confess your sins to each other and **pray** for
each other so that you may be healed.*

JAMES 5:13
*Are any of you suffering hardships? You should **pray**.
Are any of you happy?*

MATTHEW 18:19
*If two of you on earth agree about anything they
ask for, it will be done for them by my Father in heaven.*

2 CHRONICLES 7:14
*If my people who are called by my name
will humble themselves and **pray,** and seek my face . . .
I will hear from heaven.*

1 PETER 4:7
*Be alert and of sober mind so that you may **pray**.*

JAMES 1:6
*You must **believe** . . because the one who doubts
is like a wave of the sea, blown and
tossed by the wind.*

JOHN 16:23
*I tell you, my Father will give you
whatever you **ask** in my name.*

MARK 6:23
*Whatever you **ask** I will give you.*

JOHN 16:24

Ask, using my name, and you will receive.

JOHN 15:7

Ask whatever you wish, and it will be done for you.

APPENDIX: SAMPLE PRAYERS

The more you practice praying together, the more comfortable you'll become, and soon the words will flow from your heart and your conversations with God will feel authentic.

To help you reach that place of comfort, the following sample prayers may be a guide.

PRAYER FOR A HUSBAND AND WIFE

Heavenly Father, thank You for loving us.
Thank You for my [husband/wife].
Please help us to be open and honest with each other.
Help us to be kind and patient.
Teach us to show appreciation every day.
Help us to honor each other more than we honor ourselves.
Help our marriage grow stronger and stronger.

PRAYING WITH YOUNG CHILDREN

God, please help me to forgive others.
Help me to be obedient.
Help me to be happy.

Praying with a Friend

Lord, thank You for [name of friend].
Bless [name] today. Help [him/her]. Keep [him/her] safe.
Thank You that we can trust each other with
our concerns and our heart's desires.
Thank You for this gift of friendship.

Prayer for Family

God, please help my family. We need Your help
with _____.
Please direct us to the scriptures that will give us
clarity and comfort.
Show us how to place more attention on helping each other,
rather than ourselves.
Let us become encouragers for one another.

Prayer for Health

Lord, [partner's name/I] need(s) healing today.
Give [partner's name/me] the strength and
the wisdom to overcome this health issue.
Place doctors and people around [partner's name/me]
who can help.

Prayer for Employment

Lord, please lead [partner's name/me] to the perfect
employment opportunity.
Align [partner's name/me] to be at the right place
at the right time for Your will to be done.
We seek Your strength persevering and refusing
to accept discouragement.

PRAYER FOR CHILDREN

*God, I pray that You will protect [my/our] children
and watch over them every day.
Your Word says,* Start children off on the way they should
go, and even when they are old, they will
not turn from it [*Prov. 22:6, NIV*].
*Help us to guide them on the right path. Keep them safe from
any harm—physically, emotionally, and spiritually.
Send Your angels to protect them and defend them
against the Enemy.*

PRAYER FOR CERTAINTY

*God, there is uncertainty about [partner's name/my]
[finances . . . health . . . marriage].
Please help [partner's name/me] to focus on You
and not on circumstances.
I know that You will do what's best for [partner's name/me]
in every situation because Your word tells us
that ALL things work together for good.*

PRAYER FOR FAITH

*God, You are always with us. Please guide our every action.
There are times that doubt and fear creep
into [our/my] thoughts.
Help us lean on You and not on our own understanding.
Help us to focus not on our problems but on You, God.*

NOTES

INTRODUCTION

1 Matthew 21:2, NIV.

CHAPTER 1

1 Genesis 1:26, NIV.

2 Matthew 21:22, AKJV.

3 Matthew 9:27–31, NIV.

4 Matthew 8:26, NASB.

5 Matthew 8:32, NASB.

6 Isaiah 65:24, KJV.

7 Romans 4:17, ISV.

8 Mark 11:23, NASB.

9 Mark 11:24, NIV.

10 Dan Wooding, "Famed Heart Doctor Tells How a Patient Was Raised from the Dead After Prayer," *ASSIST News Service*, July 15, 2007, www.assistnews.net/Stories/2007/s07070094.htm, accessed September 1, 2014.

11 John 14:26, NIV.

12 *Life Application Study Bible* (Wheaton, IL: Tyndale House Publishers, and Grand Rapids, MI: Zondervan, 1991), 2421.

13 Ephesians 3:16, NLT.

14 Isaiah 55:11, KJV.

15 Matthew 17:20, NIV.

16 Ibid.

17 1 Corinthians 2:5, NIV.

18 Romans 10:10, NIV.

19 Matthew 21:22, ISV.

20 Lewis E. Jones, 1899.

21 Tim Keller, *Prayer* (New York: Dutton, 2014).

22 Alex Bunn and David Randall, "Health Benefits of Christian Faith," Christian Medical Fellowship, 2011, http://www.cmf.org.uk/pub lications/content.asp?context=article&id=25627, accessed May 27, 2015.

23 Isaac Newton, "General Scholium," in *Mathematical Principles of Natural Philosophy*, 1687.

24 Charles E. Hummel, *Christianity Today/History Magazine*, 1991.

25 Francis Collins, *The Language of God* (New York: Simon & Schuster, 2006), 2.

26 Ibid., 20.

27 Ibid., 30.

28 Ibid., 146.

29 Frank Tipler, *The Physics of Immortality* (New York: Doubleday, 1994), preface.

30 Wernher von Braun, http://creationsafaris.com/wgcs_4vonbraun .htm, accessed April 14, 2015.

31 Wernher von Braun, http://en.wikipedia.org/wiki/Wernher_von_ Braun.

32 Wernher von Braun, "My Faith," *American Weekly*, February 10, 1963.

33 http://www.abovetopsecret.com/forum/thread398802/pg3.

34 Walter Bradley, "The 'Just-So' Universe," quoting from William Dembski and James Kushiner, *Signs of Intelligence*, 168.

35 Allan Sandage, "Sizing Up the Cosmos: An Astronomer's Quest," *The New York Times*, B9.

36 www.brainyquote.com/quotes/quotes/g/galileogal381320.html #I8d5PwikCl0wjjAG.99; accessed April 13, 2015.

37 www.brainyquote.com/search_results.html#rgZASU0ks5qzh EK2.99.

38 Ephesians 6:11, NASB.

39 John F. Kennedy, Inaugural Address, January 20, 1961, http://www .ushistory.org/documents/ask-not.htm, accessed May 26, 2015.

40 Robert Kennedy, www.brainyquote.com/quotes/authors/r/robert _kennedy.html#AuoCVT4pkyQjyQRU.99; ibid.

41 Neil Armstrong, www.brainyquote.com/quotes/quotes/n/neilarm str101137.html; ibid.

42 Drew Hansen, "Mahalia Jackson, and King's Improvisation," *The New York Times,* http://www.nytimes.com/2013/08/28/opinion/mahalia -jackson-and-kings-rhetorical-improvisation.html?_r=0.

CHAPTER 2

1 Matthew 6:13, NIV.

2 Luke 11:1, NIV.

3 Luke 12:7, AKJ.

4 Matthew 10:30, NLT.

5 Matthew 10:31, NLT.

6 Psalms 37:23, NLT.

7 1 Peter 5:7, NIV.

8 Philippians 4:19, NIV.

9 Psalms 37:4, NIV.

10 C. Austin Miles (1868–1946), written 1912, published by Word Music, LLC; Rodeheaver Co. (a division of Word, Inc.).

11 Psalms 46:10, NIV.

12 Isaiah 26:20, NIV.

13 John 10:27, NIV.

14 Ecclesiastes 4:12, NIV.

15 Al Kasha, *Reaching the Morning After* (Nashville: Thomas Nelson, 1986), 142–43.

16 Kasha, 152.

17 Al Kasha and Joel Hirschhorn, "The Morning After," 20th Century Recordings, May 1973.

18 1 Corinthians 13:12, NASB.

19 Deuteronomy 31:6, NIV.

20 Luke 18:1, NIV.

21 Galatians 6:9, NIV.

22 Psalms 91:15, ISV.

23 http://izquotes.com/quote/385543.

24 Dr. Charles Stanley, personal interview, June 2, 2010.

25 James 5:16, NASB.

CHAPTER 3

1 Matthew 18:19, NIV.

2 Philippians 4:6, NIV.

3 Psalms 46:10, NIV.

4 Pam Jacks.

5 Kesleigh Castle, http://www.kescastle.blogspot.com/, June 8, 2008.

6 Tim Conway as told to SQuire Rushnell; "Tim's Amazing Story"; *When God Winks at You* (Nashville: Thomas Nelson, 2006), 7–11.

7 Matthew, 18:3, NIV.

8 Robert and Tim Brawling are pseudonyms.

9 Pauletta Washington, in a personal interview with the authors, 12/20/07.

10 Proverbs 22:6, NIV.

11 Marian Chadwick, CBN TV, http://www.cbn.com/tv/3718999226001, accessed April 26, 2015.

12 Marian Chadwick, interview with authors, September 3, 2014.

13 Acts 1:8, NIV.

14 Hebrews 1:11, KJV; Word.

15 Romans 4:17, ISV.

16 2 Corinthians 5–7, NIV.

17 Ephesians 6:16, NIV.

18 King James Bible Dictionary, http://av1611.com/kjbp/kjv-dictionary
    /patience.html, accessed April 23, 2015.

19 Psalms 46:10, NIV.

20 Psalms 149:4, KJV 2000.

21 Faith Is Now, http://faithisnow.net/why-testimonies/, accessed April
    23, 2015.

22 1 Samuel 17:37, NIV.

CHAPTER 4

1 Jim Cymbala, *Fresh Wind, Fresh Fire* (Grand Rapids, MI: Zondervan, 1997), p. 11.

2 Ibid., p. 17.

3 Ibid., p. 25.

4 Psalms 91:11–12, NIV.

5 Hebrews 13:2, NIV.

6 "Guardian Angels Are Here, Say Most Americans," *Time*, Sept. 18,
   2008, http://content.time.com/time/nation/article/0,8599,1842179,00.html.

7 Revelation 22:8–9, NIV.

8 Charles Finney, http://topfamousquotes.com/charles-grandison-fin
   ney-quotes-on-pray/, accessed August 18, 2015.

CHAPTER 5

1 Steven Waldman, *Founding Faith* (New York: Random House, 2008),
   127–28.

2 David Barton, *Bulletproof George Washington* (Aledo, TX: WallBuilders, 1990), 12.

3 David Barton, *Founding Fathers on Prayer*, May 1, 2013, http://www .wallbuilders.com/libissuesarticles.asp?id=144096, accessed May 31, 2015.

4 Ibid., quoting: Benjamin Rush, *Letters of Benjamin Rush*, L. H. Butterfield, ed. (Princeton, NJ: American Philosophical Society, 1951), vol. I, p. 475, to Elias Boudinot on July 9, 1788.

5 Ibid., quoting: Alexander Hamilton, John Jay, James Madison, and Other Men of Their Time, *The Federalist and Other Contemporary Papers on the Constitution of the United States*, E. H. Scott, ed. (New York: Scott, Foresman, 1894), 646, Alexander Hamilton to Mr. Childs, Wednesday, October 17, 1787.

6 Ibid., quoting: Alexander Hamilton, John Jay, and James Madison, *The Federalist* (Philadelphia: Benjamin Warner, 1818), 194, James Madison, *Federalist #37*.

7 Ibid., quoting: Abraham Lincoln, *Complete Works of Abraham Lincoln*, John G. Nicolay and John Hay, eds. (New York: Tandy-Thomas, 1894), vol. VIII, pp. 235–36, "Proclamation Appointing a National Fast Day," March 30, 1863.

8 David Barton, *Bulletproof George Washington*, 8.

9 Barton, 11.

10 Barton, 24.

11 Barton, 35–36.

12 Barton, 38–42.

13 Barton, 44.

14 Barton, 49–51.

15 Barton, 53.

16 Barton, 54.

17 Barton, 56–57.

18 David Barton, Basic Data from Department of Health and Human Services, *Original Intent* (Aledo, TX: Wallbuilder Press, 2008).

19 Barton, ibid.; Basic Data from the Centers for Disease Control and Prevention and the Department of Health and Human Services.

20 Carlo D'Este, *Eisenhower: A Soldier's Life* (New York: Henry Holt, 2002), 41.

21 Grace Perkins Oursler, *Reader's Digest School Reader/Guideposts*; 1959, 9; David Barton; *Dwight D. Eisenhower*, http://www.wall builders.com/libissuesarticles.asp?id=148934, accessed March 4, 2015.

22 Perkins Oursler, 10.

23 Stephen Ambrose, *Eisenhower 1890–1952* (New York: Simon & Schuster), 36.

24 Ibid.

25 Perkins Oursler, 11.

26 David Barton, WallBuilders's founder and president, interview with author, Aledo, TX, January 28, 2010.

27 Ambrose, 42.

28 Ambrose, 38.

29 D'Este, 57.

30 David Barton interview.

CHAPTER 6

1 Sun Tzu, Thomas Cleary, trans., *The Art of War* (Boston: Shambhala Publications, 2005); originally published 512 BC.

2 Ephesians 6:12–13, NIV.

3 1 Peter 5:8, NIV.

4 Ephesians 6:17, NIV.

5 Ephesians 6:16, NIV.

6 Matthew 4:6, NIV.

7 Ephesians 6:14, NIV.

8 Ephesians 6:17, NIV.

9 Hebrews 4:12, NIV.

10 Matthew 16:23, NIV.

11 Matthew 4:10, NIV.

12 James 4:7, NIV.

13 John 8:32, NIV.

14 Jennifer LeClaire, *The Spiritual Warrior's Guide to Defeating Jezebel* (Baker Publishing Group, Kindle Edition, 2013), 175. 6/6/13.

15 Ibid., 16.

16 Robert Morris, Pastor, Gateway Church, Dallas, TX; http://www .gatewaynyc.com/blog/Jezebel; accessed May 15, 2015.

17 Steve Sampson, *Confronting Jezebel* (Minneapolis: Chosen Books), Ebooks 2012, 79–92.

18 LeClaire, 178.

19 Robert Morris, Pastor, Gateway Church, Dallas, TX.

CHAPTER 7

1 Hubie Synn, interview with authors, 3/28/14.

2 David Tyree, *More Than Just the Catch* (Florida: Excel Books, 2008).

3 Romans 10:17, NIV.

4 1 Kings 19:12, KJV.

5 Godwink Gathering, www.facebook.com/godwinks.

6 JT, Godwink Gathering, www.facebook.com/godwinks, posted January 13, 2013.

7 DW, Godwink Gathering, www.facebook.com/godwinks, posted June 20, 2013.

8 Susan Aguilar, Godwink Gathering, www.facebook.com/godwinks; posted June 11/13, 2013.

9 BLS, Godwink Gathering, www.facebook.com/godwinks, posted January 11, 2013.

10 Kim, Godwink Gathering, www.facebook.com/godwinks, posted May 7, 2013.

11 Alisha Gilman, Godwink Gathering, www.facebook.com/godwinks, posted March 5, 2013, and interview with authors, February 22, 2015.

12 This story had five postings seen by 118,848; 20,408; 21,824; 27,088; and 62,368 people, or a total of 250,536, March 5, 2013.

CHAPTER 8

1 Kenny and Donna McLeod, interview with authors, May 5, 2015.

2 Matthew 21:22, NET.

3 Proverbs 18:21, KJV.

4 Geoff Edwards, "Black History Month: An Interview with Roy Eaton," *Advertising Age*, February 16, 2011, http://adage.com/article /creativity-news/black-history-month-interview-roy-eaton/148896/, accessed May 10, 2015.

5 Dave Horn, "Mother's Influence Lasts a Lifetime," *Wayne Independent*, May 9, 2015, http://www.wayneindependent.com/article/20150509 /BLOGS/305099999/-1/entertainment%20life, accessed May 10, 2015.

6 Luke 8:11, NKJ.

7 Norman Vincent Peale, personal interview by the author, 1990.

8 1 Corinthians 2:5, NIV.

9 2 Corinthians 5:7, NIV.

10 Luke 1:37, KJV.

11 Ted Wueste, DM, "A Transforming Thankfulness," Desert Direction; http://desertdirection.com/2014/11/26/a-transforming-thankful ness/; accessed 8/09/15.

STUDY GUIDE

1 Matthew 21:22, NET.

2 Matthew 18:20, NLT.

3 John Rossomando, "Born-Again Christians No More Immune to

Divorce Than Others," Christianity.com, http://www.christianity
.com/1116492/, accessed June 25, 2015.

4   Matthew 21:22, NET.

5   Genesis 1:3, NIV.

6   Genesis 1:26, NIV.

7   Mark 11:24, NIV.

8   http://izquotes.com/quote/385543.

9   Hebrews 12:1–2, NIV.

10 Ephesians 6:10–18, NIV.

11 Ephesians 6:12, NIV.

12 James 4:7, NIV.

13 Ephesians 6:17, NIV.

14 Hebrews 4:12, NIV.

15 Ephesians 6:17, NIV.

16 Ephesians 6:16, NIV.

17 Romans 10:17, NIV.

ALSO BY
SQUIRE RUSHNELL
& LOUISE DUART

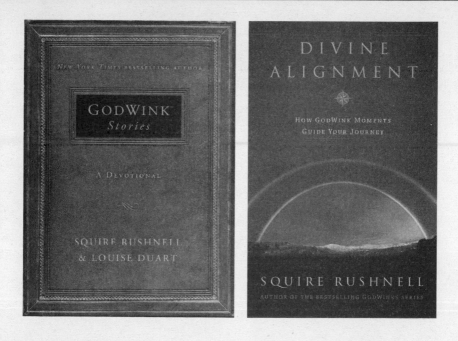

Available wherever books are sold
or at **SimonandSchuster.com**